THERE ARE about 60,000 pubs in England. Some are splendid, some dreadful, and some (in a Yorkshire phrase) fair-to-middling. Although it may be placed in any one of those categories, no pub can be relied upon to stay there. The bulldozers may have been tamed, and some fine beers reinstated to positions of proper pride, but pubs still change. The institution itself is subject to evolutionary change, with the odd hiccup, but an individual pub may alter almost overnight – especially if there is a new owner or licensee. Thus it is the pub as a phenomenon which must be sought out, not any one particular house. A single-minded journey may lead to disappointment: a pub bereft of darts or skittles, where the entertainment has been extinguished, or the kitchen razed. In such circumstances, the answer is to keep on looking. Round the corner may be an undiscovered delight, or a pub which is providing fresh pleasures under its own new management.

Several local pub guides, of varying quality, have been published. Among the more useful ones are those produced for various towns by the Campaign for Real Ale (34 Alma Road, St Albans, Hertfordshire). A broader guide to pubs is *Beers of Britain,* by Conal Gregory and Warren Knock (Cassell/Johnston and Bacon, 1975). Frank Baillie's *Beer Drinker's Companion* (David and Charles, 1974), a boon to the real enthusiast, concerns itself primarily with breweries. The best-known of England's ale-fanciers, Richard Boston, shares his experiences, flavoured with advice and anecdotes, in *Beer and Skittles* (Collins, 1976).

Other aspects of the pub have been thoroughly covered by experts in those particular fields. Timothy Finn's *Pub Games of England* (Queen Anne Press, 1975) is one entertaining example. Among sources on pubs' names, Eric Delderfield has been particularly prolific, with works like *Inns and Their Signs* (David and Charles, 1976). Brian Spiller's *Victorian Public Houses* (David and Charles, 1972) is an enjoyable and informative work of history. Although Spiller concentrates on London, he has a few welcome words on the Dublin version of the pub – which, as he properly explains, is a different thing altogether. The erudite Mark Girouard's *Victorian Pubs* (Studio Vista, 1975) is an authoritative architectural study, again concentrating on London.

I am especially indebted to Robert Thorne, of the Greater London Council's Historic Buildings Department, for his guidance. Thorne has made detailed studies of Victorian pub life in Liverpool and Birmingham. His *Birmingham Pubs*, written with Alan Crawford, was published in 1975 by the Urban and Regional Studies Centre at that city's university. For access to earlier works and information, I am grateful to various collections, especially the London Library, the British Museum, the Victoria and Albert, the Department of the Environment, the National Monument Record, and the Royal Institute of British Architects' library. The collectors and theatre historians Joe Mitchenson and Raymond Mander, whose works include *British Music Hall* (Gentry Books, 1974), have been of great help.

More than anyone, Bob Webber, of the Brewers' Society, has unearthed information and answered questions with care and patience. Almost every one of England's breweries has gone to great lengths to help. Despite my efforts to ensure that they should, one or two estimable breweries did not find a place in these pages, but their beers will continue to be appreciated. I have been critical of the past performances of some large brewing groups, but it has given me greater pleasure to record their more recent changes of emphasis. A great many publicans have helped, of course, and their profession will always have my financial support.

Thanks, too, to Mr R. F. Bryant and his colleagues at Gaskell and Chambers, makers of beer-engines; Mr W. R. Farmer and his colleagues at Buller's, makers of pump-handles in pottery; Mr C. Chalk and his colleagues at Clark and Eaton, who make decorated glass for pubs; and to my wife Maggie O'Connor for all of her help, but especially her advice on the decor and arts of the early 20th century.

I am deeply grateful to Hugh Van Dusen, whose idea this was. My thanks also to John Marmaras, Midge Keator and Woody Camp for their help in New York; and to the O'Connors and McGovrens for theirs, beneath Ben Bulben, in County Sligo, Ireland.

M.J.

Picture Credits: End paper, Ian Howes; Page 2, Jon Wyand; 3, Robert Morley; 4, Iain Macmillan; 5, The Licensed Victualler's Gazette; 6, Roger Daniels; 8, The Licensed Victualler's Gazette; 9, Mary Evans (top) and Ian Howes; 10–11, Jon Wyand; 12–13, Ian Howes (all); 14, Victoria & Albert/Jon Wyand; 15, Whitbread and Victoria & Albert (The George), David Brinson (The Globe); 16, Brewers' Society; 17, Mary Evans; 18, Red Lion; 19, Roger Daniels; 20–21, Eldridge, Pope; 22, Mander and Mitchenson Theatre Collection; 23, Ian Howes (except Ladies' Bar, Jon Wyand); 24, Trevor Wood; 25, Brewers' Society (Kitchener) and Ian Howes; 26, 28, Ian Howes; 29, Brewers' Society; 30, Brewers' Society and Mary Evans (White Hart); 31, Patrick Thurston; 32, Brewers' Society; 33, Stanley Chew (Cross Keys), Whitbread (Hope and Anchor), Ian Howes; 34, 35, 36, Ian Howes; 37, Stanley Chew (Henry VIII, Charles II), Brewers' Society (Henry VII), Whitbread (Henry VI), Ian Howes (Victoria), Robert Morley (Blackboy's); 38, Stanley Chew; 39–43 Ian Howes (all); 44, Museum of London; 45, EMI; 46, Trevor Wood; 47, The Licensed Victualler's Gazette; 48, Ian Howes; 49, The Licensed Victualler's Gazette; 50–51, Jon Wyand; 52, 53, Ian Howes; 54–55, Iain Macmillan (colour) and Gaskell & Chambers; 56, Ian Howes; 57 (McMullen's), Trevor Wood; 58–59, Jon Wyand; 60, Iain Macmillan; 61, Ian Howes; 62, Pike & Musket; 63, Ian Howes; 64, 65, 66, Brewers' Society; 67, Trevor Wood; 68–72, Ian Howes (all); 73, Colorific; 74–75, Courtauld Institute and Bass Charrington; 76–77, Collection Stewart Cropper/Jon Wyand; 78–79, Ridley's Brewery; 81–81, Guinness; 82–83, Brewers' Society; 84–85, Roger Daniels (Adnams'), Trevor Wood (McMullen's); 86–89, breweries; 90–92, Ian Howes; 93, Iain Macmillan; 94, Architectural Review; 95, Ian Howes; 96–97, The Builder; 98–101, Ian Howes (all); 102, The Licensed Victualler's Gazette; 103, Ian Howes; 104, Patrick Thurston (top) and Courage's; 105, British Tourist Authority and Ian Howes (Clickham Inn); 106–109, Ian Howes, Mary Evans, Stanley Chew (sign); 110, Ian Howes; 112, Brewers' Society; 113, Evening Echo, Southend; 115, Ian Howes; 116, Courage's; 117, The Licensed Victualler's Gazette; 118, Mary Evans; 119, English Tourist Board; 120, breweries; 121, Roger Daniels; 122, Ian Howes; 124, Radio Times Hulton Picture Library (shove ha'penny) and Mansell Collection; 125, Ian Howes (cribbage); 126, Ian Howes (pool) and The Licensed Victualler's Gazette; 127, Ian Howes; 128–9, Keystone (hood game) **and AP**; 130, Martin Richardson; 131, Ian Howes; 132, The Licensed Victualler's **Gazette; 133, Iain** Macmillan; 134, Mander and Mitchenson (Limerick Races) and The Licensed Victualler's Gazette; 135, Ian Howes; 136–7, Mander and Mitchenson and aba daba music-hall (Pindar of Wakefield); 138, Trevor Wood; 140, Radio Times Hulton Picture Library; 142–3, Richard Cooke; 144, Valerie Wilmer; 146, Ian Howes; 148, Mary Evans; 149, Iain Macmillan; 150, The Licensed Victualler's Gazette; 151, Roger Daniels/Robert Morley; 152, Radio Times Hulton Picture Library; 153, Ian Howes; 155, Collection Maggie O'Connor; 156, Brewers' Society; 157, The Guildhall Library; 158, Trevor Wood; 160, Radio Times Hulton Picture Library; 162–3, breweries; 164–7, Ian Howes (all); 168, Robert Morley (top) and Iain Macmillan.

A QUARTO BOOK

THE ENGLISH PUB

Michael Jackson

HARPER & ROW, PUBLISHERS

New York, Evanston, Hagerstown, San Francisco

Country pub near Southwaite, Cumbria

Contents

A QUARTO BOOK
Designed and produced by Jackson Morley Publishing Ltd,
20 Kingly Street, London W1, England

Edited and written by Michael Jackson and Frank Smyth. Design and
art direction by Robert Morley and Roger Daniels. Original
photography by Ian Howes, Iain Macmillan, Trevor Wood and Jon
Wyand. Editorial Consultant Patrick Roper. Research by Susan van
Tijn and Diana James. Production by Bison Books.

© 1976 Jackson Morley Publishing Ltd

Filmset by Jolly & Barber Ltd, Rugby, England
Printed by Dai Nippon Printing Company Ltd, Tokyo, Japan

First US Edition

Library of Congress Catalog Card Number 75-25053

ISBN: 0-06-102179-3

76 77 78 79 80 10 9 8 7 6 5 4 3 2 1

A Unique Phenomenon

The role of the English pub

'PUB' is as English as a word can be. A familiarization to describe the most familiar place in the neighbourhood. Who would be so formal as to say 'public house'? Yet it was once a house, where the public were guests of the host and hostess. The best of pubs still are, their success depending upon the popularity of the landlord and landlady. The host and hostess on the left are the landlord and landlady at the Queen Adelaide pub, in Battersea, London. Above, the Napier, High Holborn, London, at the turn of the century.

THE PUB is an institution unique to England, and there is nothing more English. It is not an American bar, darkened still by the long shadow of Prohibition; not a French café, where people sunnily drink aperitifs on the pavement; not a Bavarian beer-hall, full of swaying and noise.

Other countries have royal families, parliaments, and double-decker buses, but only England has pubs. Kings and queens of England, dukes and earls, provide a venue for a pint; the occasional politician is hung outside licensed premises (London has its liberal Charles James Fox in Soho, and its socialist Clement Attlee in Fulham, to name but two); London buses and trains announce that they are going to the *Angel*, the *Elephant and Castle* or the *Royal Oak*. Everyone knows what they mean, even if their choice of pubs may be questioned.

In New York and Tokyo, Hamburg and Paris, there are 'pubs' called the *Britannia*, the *Sir Winston Churchill* and suchlike, but they are not English. Despite honourable efforts, the pub has not been successfully transplanted into other countries, because it is an organic part of the growth of English community life. It has taken centuries to develop, in an English soil whose many troubles have still been fewer than those of neighbouring lands. Not only does the pub belong to an island race, it has only half-heartedly spread itself beyond the Black Mountains to Wales and the Cheviot Hills to Scotland – and, notwithstanding Dublin's claims, has hardly bothered to cross the sea to Ireland.

The pub is even more English than *Punch* magazine – conceived in the Fleet Street tavern which now bears its name. More English even than cricket – developed in a pub now known as the *Bat and Ball*, at Hambledon, Hampshire. Eccentric humour can be enjoyed elsewhere in the world, cricket's arcane rituals have established themselves in other lands, but the pub is exclusively English.

That is not to say that foreigners cannot benefit from the

In the country especially, the pub is an organic part of the community . . . the Harbour Inn, Southwold, Suffolk.

pub; it has offered its hospitality to ideas and philosophies which have helped change the world.

Both Marx and Lenin are said to have refreshed their intellects at the *Pindar of Wakefield*, in Gray's Inn Road, London, better known in more recent times for its music-hall and jazz. Thomas Paine, on the other hand, called the English pub 'the cradle of American independence.' He wrote *The Rights of Man* in the same part of London, at the *Old Red Lion*, St John Street, Clerkenwell. He also founded his radical discussion group The Headstrong Club at the *White Hart*, in Lewes, Sussex. George III's son Prince Augustus Frederick was so attracted to the *Dove*, a riverside pub in Hammersmith, London, that he bought part of it as a 'smoking box' where he could relax while working on his favourite cause, the abolition of the slave trade. In the same four walls, the nationalistic song *Rule Britannia* was written by a Scot, James Thomson, whose name is more often connected with his poem *The Four Seasons*.

The poet's ability to cope with the elements was called into question by his death from a chill caught while taking a boat across the Thames, but the *Dove* survives and flourishes, one of the many pubs protected by order of the Department of the Environment. The *Dove* also exemplifies the hundreds of pubs which claim historic and literary significance, though few with such eclecticism. It stands conveniently next door to the home of William Morris, the 19th-century socialist writer and designer, with an historic publishing house on the other side, and claims to have been patronized by Ernest Hemingway and Graham Greene.

The Greene family set an excellent example in the further-ance of the links between pubs and the literary establishment. Graham's brother, Sir Hugh Greene, is best known as a former director-general of the BBC. (In his time there, British broad-casting was revolutionized, the slings and arrows of a new gen-eration of satirists let loose). But Sir Hugh is also a critic, writer, publisher . . . and chairman of the East Anglian country brew-ery Greene, King. As a knight, Sir Hugh, as British as the BBC, is in good company among the prefixed ranks of the brewers – mockingly known as 'The Beerage.' As a man of words, he more properly belongs on the other side of the bar. Clearly he is not without sympathy for the community of beer-drinkers, who have often had cause to see the brewers as their natural enemy, forever tampering with pubs and beer alike. Although Sir Hugh's firm has its critics among connoisseurs of beer, he was, paradoxically, an early shareholder in a company set up by the preservationist Campaign for Real Ale with the object of running pubs inde-pendently from the brewers. A real British compromise.

The controversy over brewers and beers assumed new pass-ion in the late 1960s and early 1970s, when pubs were subject to an assault of 'modernization.' It was even argued that newfangled methods of serving beer, apart from impairing the drink, were diminishing the barmaid as a proper object for the lust of every red-blooded and glassy-eyed Englishman. In defence of traditional serving methods, the following rhyme was published in the *New Statesman*: 'Not turning taps, but pulling pumps, gives barmaids splendid busts and rumps.' Hardly the sort of sentiment that motivated Beatrice and Sidney Webb when they founded the socialist journal. Another curator of the liberal conscience, *The Guardian* for a time devoted a weekly column to the preservation of the best in English pubs – mindful, no doubt, of their crucial role in society.

The pub is neutral ground. The Englishman is jealous of his home: it is, after all, proverbially his castle. But castles are not always comfortable. Nor are they places in which to entertain an enemy, or even an acquaintance of questionable loyalties. A pub is not a home, but it is a house – a public house.

The reticent Englishman can invite an acquaintance for a drink in a pub without any risk that the style of his home-life will be found wanting, that clashes of class-attitude will become frontal. Nor will there be any problems in getting rid of a tiresome guest – the person who issued the invitation in the first

THE SPLENDID contribution of barmaids to the success of the English pub has long been appreciated, as evidenced by the idealized illustration from the 1850s, and the five prizewinners from the turn of the century. Were barmaids really better-looking in the old days? Drinkers at a busy lunchtime pub in Central London (right) might not agree. Pubs should be warm and welcoming places at all times, and especially on winter's evenings. A Christmas-card pose seems appropriate to a pub called the Coach and Horses (over page), despite its location in London's commuter-belt, at Ickenham.

place is at liberty to excuse himself when he wishes, providing it is not his turn to buy a round of drinks. The public house is an institution which will not compromise the Englishman's courtesy, nor will it cramp his individualistic wish to go as he pleases. In a country pub, a poacher can meet a gamekeeper with impunity. In a city pub, a business deal can be transacted without either negotiating party having the advantage of home ground. Members of Parliament representing opposing parties can discuss their differences over a beer, knowing that their 'local,' the *St Stephen's Tavern*, is fitted with a bell which will summon them back to the House of Commons if their vote is needed.

Courts have been held in pubs, and some retain evidence of the fact. Magistrates at Smithfield, London, heard cases in the *Hand and Shears* (commonly known as the *Fist and Clippers*). At Falkingham, in Lincolnshire, the *Greyhound* has holes where a portable dock was fixed. Guilty men were hanged from the beams of the *Hare and Hounds* at Newport, Isle of Wight, and the *Elm Tree*, in the delightfully-named Dorset village of Langton Herring. The *Durham Ox*, confusingly situated in Derbyshire, at Ilkeston, used to be a prison. Small wonder that British hangmen

JUDGMENT DAY . . . the final roll-call, at the Blue Anchor, Helston, Cornwall (below). Many an impetuous young man was publicly hanged in the Duchy during the 1800s. Two were executed for sheep-stealing, and one for highway robbery. The cell at the City Arms, in Wells, Somerset (bottom picture) remained in use until 1810.

have been known to become licensees, thus consolidating the connection between publicans and sinners. Thankfully, hanging has been abolished, though there are as many long-faced publicans than ever there were. At least a drinker is free to escape to somewhere more cheerful.

The Britons were 'accustomed to gathering in their ale-houses to govern and adjudicate' as long ago as the first century A.D., according to a Greek commentator of the period, Dioscorides. Along with the tavernae set up earlier by the Romans for the sale of wine to their soldiers, the Saxon ale shops were among the progenitors of the pub.

England's drinking laws, which have gradually festooned the pub in a tangle of confusion, started with the Saxons, too. King Edgar ordered that drinking-horns be marked with pegs, measuring each swallow, and that no one take more than a single draught at a time. Like almost all those who have since sought to restrict drinking, King Edgar merely encouraged it, by giving the zest of precision to drinking contests. The custom was revived as 'pin-drinking' by Georgian bucks, and allegedly passed into the language the expression 'to take (someone) down a peg or two.'

The rituals of drinking have grown through the ages, sometimes colourful, sometimes subtle. Like rituals in any social situation, they have woven themselves into a protective wrap of security for those taking part. The practice of buying rounds in strict rotation is the most basic example, or the custom of setting pub clocks ten minutes fast (this cannot be relied upon). Northerners expect straight-sided glasses, without handles (sometimes called schooners), dismissing the barrel-shaped handle-glass as being suitable only for effete Southerners. This last theme has

BODY AND SOUL can be refreshed in next-door establishments all over England. Just three examples (from top): The Crown, Melton Mowbray, Leicestershire; the City Tavern, Newcastle-upon-Tyne; the Old Pack Horse, Failsworth, Manchester.

countless local variations: some of Manchester's drinkers claim that handle-glasses are fit to be used only in the twin city of Salford, and accordingly dismiss them as 'Salford glasses.' The landlord who places a tea-towel over his beer-pumps at closing, after shouting, 'Time, gentlemen, please,' is observing another pub ritual. Drinkers have their own rituals, involving their own particular seat in the pub, their own personal pewter tankard, or their regular daily drink. A London television station reported that a local centenarian who visited his pub every day had walked as far as the earth is round: 25,000 miles.

Colin Wilson, who became one of the 'Angry Young Men' generation of British writers in the 1950s, with his book *The Outsider*, has since turned his attention to the question of English drinking habits. Talking, for example, about his own father, he asks: 'How can I explain why he dislikes moving from pub to pub? He says it is a waste of good drinking time; but this cannot be true, because he may sit for an hour with the same pint in front of him.' Why isn't Mr Wilson Sr. a pub-crawler? 'The real reason, I suspect, is that he feels that movement from pub to pub indicates an attitude of frivolity towards the drinking ritual. A churchgoer would feel the same about visiting several churches on a Sunday morning and staying ten minutes in each.'

The church and the pub have been linked by other writers. William Golding, author of *Lord of the Flies*, writes in *Free Fall*: 'I kept my drinking from Beatrice because she thought of pubs as only one degree less damned than the Church of England.' Or, more oblique, Joyce Cary, in *The Horse's Mouth*: 'It was a swing door. You can't bang a pub door. The pubs know a lot, almost as much as the churches.'

Some pubs have even been known to feature hymn-singing: one example is the *Pot and Lobster* in the little fishing town of Whitby, North Yorkshire; another is the *Ship Inn*, Mousehole, Cornwall. Several are actually attached to churches; the *Old Deanery*, in Ripon, also North Yorkshire, is joined to the cathedral there. Early churches took so long to build that 'hospices' were first erected alongside the site for the rest and relaxation of the construction workers. Thus the church and pub stand side by side in the geometry of the traditional English village, with their roles as meeting places inter-connecting. In large parishes, the hospice might later be used to accommodate people from remote districts who had come to attend services. The 'Church House Inn' would have a brewhouse attached, manned by monks. As Christianity spread in England, pilgrims started trekking along the old Roman roads to shrines at places like Glastonbury, Winchester (tomb of St Swithin) or, after the assassination of Thomas à Becket in 1170, Canterbury.

Pilgrims like Chaucer's were able to eat, drink and sleep at hospices set up by abbeys and priories on the road. The (Saint) *George and Pilgrims* at Glastonbury, built by Abbot John de

Selwood in 1475, is a well-known example. In another such inn, the *Angel and Royal*, at Grantham, Lincolnshire, King John is said to have held court before signing the Magna Carta. The inn claims to be the oldest in England, and some of its cellar masonry dates back to 1213.

When Henry VIII dissolved the monasteries in the sixteenth century, the duties of inn-keeping passed to the lay gentry, the Lords of the Manor. Ecclesiastical signs gave way to heraldic names, like the *Red Lion*, the *White Horse*, or the more fanciful *Bear and Ragged Staff*. Some of these inns were the size of small country houses, and were run by the owner's estate stewards, or 'landlords,' and a new word was introduced into the vocabulary of English drinking.

Strolling players, among them Shakespeare himself, came on to the scene at the end of the Tudor period. Inns added entertainment to their services, the performance taking place in the courtyard while guests watched from a surrounding gallery. This arrangement, which conditioned early theatre design in England, can be seen at the *George*, in Borough High Street, Southwark, London. The *George*, built in the 1600s, is one of several pubs now owned by the National Trust.

'Vulgar and tavern music' was frowned upon by the puritans, but they still found the evil inns to be necessary. Oliver Cromwell himself is associated with at least half a dozen pubs which still exist, and the *Sun*, at Hitchin, Hertfordshire, served as his army headquarters for some time.

The Turnpike Act of 1663 and the inauguration of mail coaches in 1784 provided a last and spectacular fling for the inn. Post-houses, or coaching inns, established themselves as important features of towns all over England. Dr Johnson made his often-quoted remark: 'No sir, there is nothing which has yet been contrived by man, by which so much happiness is produced as by a good tavern or inn.'

The coming of the railways in the 1830s and 1840s greatly diminished the importance of inns, though the surfacing of roads and the spread of private carriages prevented some from disappearing altogether. The great coaching inns, especially those at termini, had sold travel tickets, and been meeting places in much the way that railway stations would become; they had also sown the seed of the big, city pub.

England's drinking habits were experiencing changes, too. Coffee, tea and chocolate had been brought to England by the era of exploration. Pepys had recorded that he drank tea for the first time in 1660. The coffee house had become widespread, though Defoe observed of the large number he saw in Shrewsbury in 1714: 'When you come into them, they are but alehouses, only they think that the name of coffee-house gives them a better air.' Reeling from public derision after attempting to pioneer a device called the umbrella, one Jonas Hanway tried to

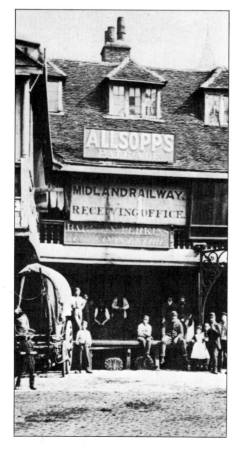

TRAVEL CENTRE: *The most famous of all inns was the Tabard, whence Chaucer's pilgrims set out from London to Canterbury. An inn survived on the site in Borough High Street, Southwark, until 1875/6. As coaching declined, the management of the establishment showed considerable commercial dexterity; in the last decade of its life (below), the inn was one of several that acted as parcels offices for the burgeoning railways. There had once been a number of renowned inns in Borough High Street, among them the White Hart, featured in Shakespeare's Henry VI and Dickens' Pickwick Papers.*

PLAYING TO THE GALLERY . . . HOW THE INN FATHERED THE THEATRE

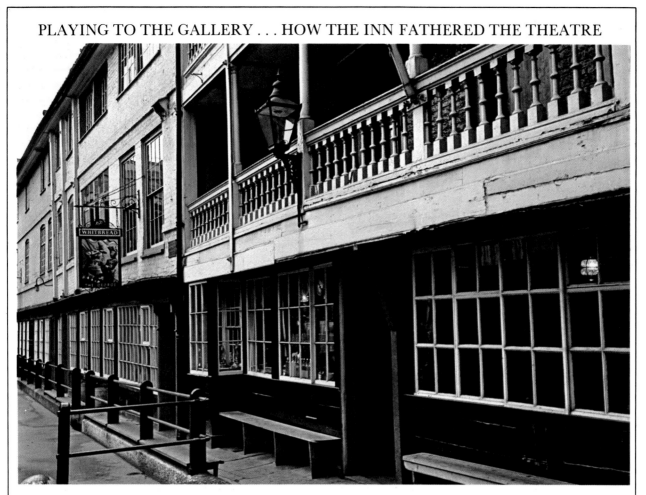

SHAKESPEARE'S Globe Theatre derived its layout from the inn-yard, where strolling players could be watched from galleries.
One 17th-century hostelry in Borough High Street, the George, came close to an ironic end. Soon after the photograph on the right was taken, part of the inn was demolished in 1889 to make room for a railway. The rest of the George survives, and functions as a pub (top picture).

DEMOCRATS! Guard Your Liberty!

BRITISH
LIBERTY
OAK

LOCAL
VETO

**Your Freedom is being attacked
by teetotal fanatics, who want
to force you to conform to their
own narrow habits of life.**

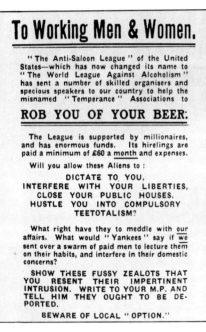

To Working Men & Women.

"The Anti-Saloon League" of the United
States—which has now changed its name to
"The World League Against Alcoholism"
has sent a number of skilled organisers and
specious speakers to our country to help the
misnamed "Temperance" Associations to

ROB YOU OF YOUR BEER:

The League is supported by millionaires,
and has enormous funds. Its hirelings are
paid a minimum of £60 a month and expenses.

Will you allow these Aliens to:

DICTATE TO YOU,
INTERFERE WITH YOUR LIBERTIES,
CLOSE YOUR PUBLIC HOUSES,
HUSTLE YOU INTO COMPULSORY
TEETOTALISM?

What right have they to meddle with our
affairs. What would "Yankees" say if we
sent over a swarm of paid men to lecture them
on their habits, and interfere in their domestic
concerns?

SHOW THESE FUSSY ZEALOTS THAT
YOU RESENT THEIR IMPERTINENT
INTRUSION. WRITE TO YOUR M.P. AND
TELL HIM THEY OUGHT TO BE DE-
PORTED.

BEWARE OF LOCAL "OPTION."

*AMERICANS influenced temperance
agitation in Britain right from the start, with
seamen distributing literature in the port of
Liverpool as early as 1829. American influence
was still at work in 1920, when – with the
United States introducing Prohibition – the
temperance movement in Britain was on its last
legs. For half a century, Britain had debated
the possibility of district votes on liquor laws
('local veto' or 'local option'). The measure
had finally been passed by the Commons only to
be thrown out by the Lords. Whatever
England's view, the other countries of the
British Isles always seemed more amenable to
such ideas, and a form of local option still
exists in Wales. A more tangible reminder of
those argumentative days is the odd surviving
temperance building. The coffee 'tavern'
on the right, called the Lamb and Flag, was
built at Redruth, Cornwall, in 1880.*

reinstate himself by attacking another unEnglish custom: 'Were
they the sons of tea-sippers who won the fields of Crécy and
Agincourt, or dyed the Danube's shores with Gallic blood?' The
coffee-house would re-appear more than a century and a half
later, as part of the temperance phenomenon, and be dismissed
even more rapidly.

The temperance wagon would ultimately be set rolling by
another new drink, originally intended to counter foreign imports. The Irish and Scots were already producing spirits for
their own consumption in the 16th century, and in 1690 an Act of
Parliament was passed giving every citizen the right to distil
liquor from English-grown corn. When William of Orange had
come from the Low Countries to take the British throne, the
Dutch drink of gin had come with him, and this was what the
English distilled. Beer had already become subject to substantial
duties, and the flood of untaxed gin led to 'dram-shops' being set
up by the thousand in London. There were 9,000 gin-shops in
the city by 1740.

Hogarth's drawings *Gin Lane* and *Beer Street* contrasted the
degradation brought about by the insidious spirit with the robust
cheer of the traditional English drink, which Member of Parliament Henry Brougham later described as 'a moral species of
beverage.' A century of drunkenness had all but been brought
under control by propaganda and legislation when the Duke of
Wellington launched a new initiative ostensibly intended to

REDRUTH TEMPERANCE HALL & COFFEE TAVERN,

IS AN IMPOSING BUILDING ERECTED BY PUBLIC SUBSCRIPTION FROM THE DESIGNS OF Mr HICKS, ARCHITECT.
IT WAS OPENED MAY, 13TH 1880, BY LADY JANE VIVIAN, AND IS OF COMMANDING APPEARANCE. THE GROUND-FLOOR
IS FITTED UP AS A COFFEE TAVERN AND TEMPERANCE RESTAURANT ON THE NEWEST PRINCIPLE, WHILE THE UPPER PORTION
OF THE BUILDING CONSISTS OF A SPACIOUS HALL OR LECTURE ROOM, CAPABLE OF SEATING NEARLY 200 PERSONS.

HOGARTH'S famous engravings contrasting the degradation in Gin Lane (left) with the robust content of Beer Street. The spirit was a massive problem in Hogarth's time, much more so than in the 'Gin-Palace' era more than a century later. To combat imports of brandy, every Englishman had been given the right to distil and sell spirits. In the 1730s, masters were even paying their workpeople in gin. Beer, on the other hand, had been heavily taxed by William of Orange to finance his activities in Ireland.

draw drinkers away from gin. He freed beer from licensing laws and from duty, and his Act of 1830 predictably had the opposite effect of that supposedly intended. In a year, 30,000 new 'beer-shops' sprung up, and the established licensed houses hit back by revamping themselves into what became known as 'gin-palaces.'

Some of these houses were already owned by breweries, and others soon would be. No longer were brewhouse and alehouse one and the same place; with the growth of commerce and industrial capitalism, brewing was becoming a major manufacturing activity. But, insecure over changing drinking habits, the growing breweries wanted some control over the places in which their products were sold. Their anxiety to keep a grip on their market was one factor in the evolution of the 'tied-house' system which is such a marked characteristic of English pubs. Competition among pubs was also encouraging publicans to spend money beyond their means on their establishments to attract custom. Publicans who had an arrangement to be supplied exclusively by a brewery soon found themselves borrowing money from the company, becoming mortgagees, and ultimately tenants. When drink laws were eventually tightened, licences had scarcity value, and breweries were even more keen to own houses. Later pressure by magistrates for the physical condition of pubs to be improved merely increased publicans' cash problems. In England, as in no other country, brewers would ultimately gain control over the overwhelming majority of their outlets, with tenants in the very long term being replaced by managers. The system would face continued criticism on the grounds of its being monopolistic, but the conditions which had created it would also preserve it. Samuel Whitbread already had tied houses in the 18th century, and names like Bass, Charrington, Worthington and Watney were already becoming familiar to drinkers.

As London grew and spread, landowners like the Marquis of Westminster, Felix Ladbroke and Lord Holland parcelled out their property to speculative builders, many of whom saw pubs as a good investment. In new areas like Ladbroke Grove and Holland Park pubs mushroomed. The pub now called the *Sir Winston Churchill*, in Campden Street, is a good example; the *Sun in Splendour*, Pembridge Road, is another. These purpose-built pubs were the first urban 'locals.' The journal *The Builder* talked in 1854 about, 'a tavern of imposing elevation standing quite complete, waiting the approaching rows of houses.' The journal observed: 'At a distance of 200 paces in every direction, they glitter in sham splendour. The object of erecting them is to obtain a larger sum than the builder can acquire for any other species of property.' The speculators built pubs half a dozen at a time, sometimes using them as canteens for their workers while the rest of the development went on. They obtained licences, then sold or rented to what *The Builder* described as 'adventuring publicans.' Sometimes the speculative builders, having once involved themselves in the business, became publicans. Because the pub's social status was questionable, speculative builders like Thomas Cubitt hid them in mews when he developed aristocratic Belgravia, and kept them out of the squares in middle-class Pimlico.

The Industrial Revolution was in full spate and the pop-

GIN PALACE . . . surviving still, a small but superb example of the style, a few minutes' walk from Piccadilly. An archetypally-English pub scene, at the Red Lion, Duke of York Street, near St James's Square. The pub has changed little since being photographed in the late 1950s.

POOR TRUST IS DEAD.

ADNAMS
PALE ALE

ADNAMS
FINE OLD ALE

BAD PAY KILLED HIM.

TRUST, embodied in the dog, the Englishman's faithful friend. The notice refers to customers who have defaulted on credit arrangements with the landlord. A curiously over-sophisticated example of early 20th-century poster art, from a rustic house in East Anglia. A determinedly-local pub, the King's Head, at Laxfield, near Halesworth, Suffolk, recalls the original ale-house style in its bar-less interior.

ulation of cities like London was being swollen by immigrant workers from rural districts. Dickens documented the period graphically enough, and mentioned dozens of pubs in his writings. Mayhew's *London Labour and the London Poor* reported on the street vendors and entertainers, with their 'penny gaffs' acting as drunken places of amusement. The social focus and rituals of village life had been left behind, and the new city-dwellers had to find a replacement. Pubs became centres for entertainment, sport and the dissemination of information. Pubs acted as employment exchanges, sometimes let rooms (and called themselves hotels), and wages were often paid out there.

The habit would later emerge, and still exists to some extent, whereby trusted customers can get their drink on credit, and settle the 'slate' on pay-day. Many landlords have taken to displaying coy notices saying that they cannot cash cheques, but others still permit their pubs to be used as informal banks by established regulars. Weekly meetings of 'loan-clubs,' a sort of neighbourhood benefit society, are few these days, but many pubs have seaside outings for pensioners. Nor would any local newspaper get by without a picture of a pile of pennies collected for charity, being ceremonially toppled in a pub.

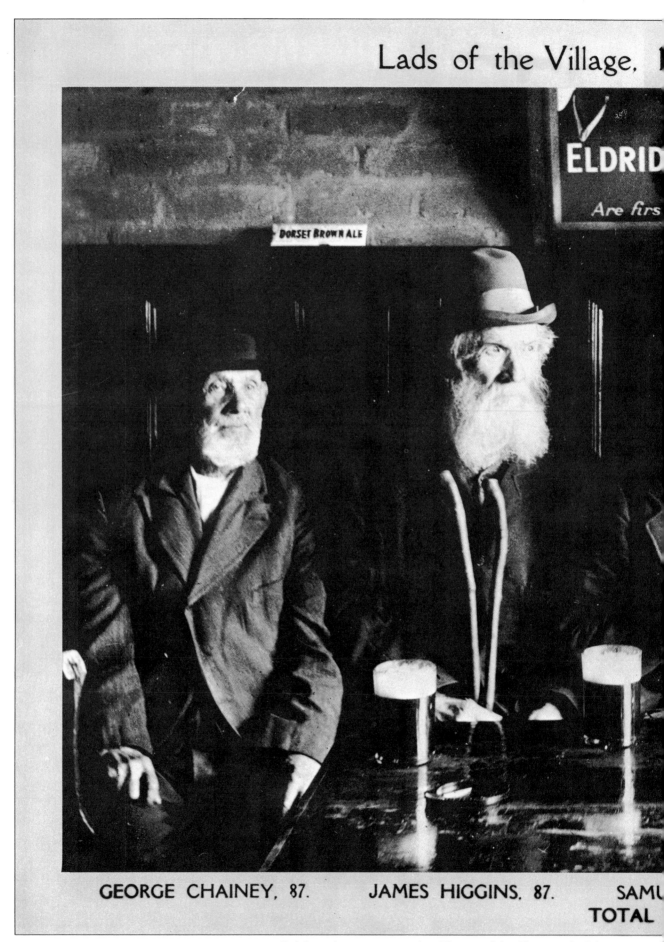

Lads of the Village,

ELDRID

Are firs

DORSET BROWN ALE

GEORGE CHAINEY, 87.   JAMES HIGGINS, 87.   SAMU
                                                    TOTAL

Drinkers who span two centuries: The sons of the village meet in their customary pl

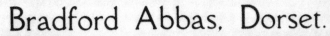

Bradford Abbas, Dorset.

G. 90.   THOMAS COOMBS. 89.   SIDNEY PARSONS. 81.

34 YEARS.

bly, to record the face of the community . . . at the Rose and Crown, Bradford Abbas, Dorset.

MUSIC-HALL comes to the West End of London: The Black Horse Inn, to the left of the picture, had a 'sing-song saloon,' which grew into the London Pavilion (to the right), 'the first music-hall de-luxe,' in 1861. It was here that the phrase 'by Jingo!' was immortalized in a chauvinistic song about the Russo-Turkish war. The music-hall was completely reconstructed in 1885, and the replacement building today houses a cinema, still called the London Pavilion. The Black Horse has gone . . . there is little need for coaching inns in Piccadilly Circus, the hub of Europe's biggest and most traffic-ridden city.

FACING PAGE: The further departmentalization of the pub. Smoke Rooms at the Bridge Hotel, Salford, Greater Manchester (also Lounge); and the Vines, Lime Street, Liverpool. Luncheon Bar at the Turk's Head ('Whitelock's'), off Briggate, Leeds. News Room at the Central, Ranelagh Street, Liverpool. Ladies' Bar at the Clachan, Kingly Street, London. Bar Parlour at the Lord Clyde, Deansgate, Manchester.

Life was less cosy in the 1880s, and the pubs had to provide escape from its inhuman realities. Entertainment was in demand to the extent the upper and back rooms were set aside for the staging of shows: thus the music-hall, another famous English institution, was spawned by the pub. More and more ambitious music-halls were attached to pubs until, by the end of the century, the variety theatre was set to establish itself as a separate institution.

The music-hall was just one aspect of the departmentalization of the pub. While some pubs had massive bars, with an island counter of the type devised by Brunel to cope with sudden crushes of customers in railway refreshment rooms, others were divided in an infinite variety of permutations: Parlours, private and public bars, tap-rooms, ladies' rooms and snugs. A range of different terms were used, and their precise meaning varied from pub to pub. Just behind Oxford Circus, opposite the Palladium is a fading example of such a pub, the *Argyll*. Several houses retain ladies' bars, though the widespread idea of men-only pubs has largely died out; neither could enforce their intended restrictions today without coming into conflict with the Sex Discrimination legislation of 1975.

The fashion for compartmentalized pubs reached its height around 1890, when some had as many as 15 'boxes.' Gradually, saloon and public bars became the main divisions, catering respectively for white-collar workers and labourers, with a 'jug-and-bottle' for off-sales. Eventually, even these distinctions would fade, with brewers in the 1960s taking advantage of contemporary social aspirations to abolish public bars and sell all drinks at the slightly higher 'saloon-bar prices.' Today, some pubs also have a lounge, in which there is waiter service.

Waiter-service had once been the custom, and the introduction of counter-service had been one factor in the growth of compartmentalization. The practice had also offered privacy to drinkers, and enabled pubs to try and accommodate a wider social range of customers. Whether it did is questionable. Small and enclosed bars invited crime the length and breadth of the country, according to magistrates of the day. Snugs were especially singled out for attack: there had been robberies in snugs in Hull, and a prostitute of 19 had robbed a man of 70 in a snug at the *Lion Hotel*, Lincoln, in 1894.

Among the upper classes, only 'bohemians' went into pubs during the late 1800s. A 96-year-old matriarch named Rosie who was still patronizing a snug in Islington, London, during the late 1960s, used to entertain drinkers with a story about one such bohemian, Oscar Wilde. She claimed she had once given Wilde sexual satisfaction when she was a teenage flower-girl. She was not a whore, she explained; she had done the deed by hand, for two pence. Most of the girls did it for 'gents,' and the practice was

known as 'tuppenny nutting.' Subsequently the term, 'I don't give a tuppenny toss' found its way into common usage.

The term 'public house' seems to have achieved official recognition in 1854, when a House of Commons Select Committee used the expression. This was the century of the pub. 'The 1890s was their golden age,' comments Mark Girouard, in his scholarly work, *Victorian Pubs*. 'The pubs then were bigger and brighter, their fittings more sumptuous than they had ever been before or were to be again.'

The moral pressures that finally curbed small bars in favour of something easier to supervize also demanded that some of the wider social functions be removed from the boozy environment of the pub. Inquests and tax-collection were no longer held in pubs, nor were election meetings. With the emergence of first the Liberals and then Labour, both sympathetic to the temperance movement, political parties no longer used pubs as local headquarters. At the same time there grew an empathy between brewers and the Conservative Party which has remained ever since. Among those who did meet in pubs were Freemasons'

WIDER FUNCTIONS: Lieutenant Ross awaited recruits at the Tumbling Sailors pub. Mr Graham afforded 'amusement and gratification to the inhabitants of Greenwich,' then asked that donations to cover his costs be lodged at the Mitre Tavern. The Ouse River Board used a pub at Denver, Norfolk, for toll-collection.

LORD KITCHENER appealed via publicans for sobriety among the Armed Forces, but the men in the trenches would have responded more readily to the call of Greenall Whitley's beer, as presented by the company's advertising artist of the time. To beleaguered troops, alcoholic reinforcements would have been as welcome as the arrival of the Cavalry in a Western movie. The Government saw things differently: drink was on the side of the enemy. The restrictions which followed have conditioned pubs' hours of business ever since.

lodges and such exotic societies as the Royal and Antediluvian Order of Buffaloes, and the Oddfellows.

A few years ago, a Midlands brewery conducted a survey into the organized activities that took place in pubs, and discovered that nearly 3,000 bodies regularly met in its houses, ranging from yacht clubs to anglers' societies, pigeon fanciers to professional rat-catchers. Country pubs are often a regular venue for the County Show committee, city pubs for trade union branches. Boxers train in gyms attached to pubs, bands practise in upstairs rooms, and fringe theatre groups perform in the lounge. Community action groups have made videotape presentations in pubs to arouse local opinion over issues, and street festivals have been planned there. And no pub would be worthy of the name without a regular visit from the Salvation Army – another institution that blossomed at the end of the 19th century.

The last act in the creation of the English pub as it is known today came with the first decades of the 20th century. Of all the laws passed over the centuries to determine what may and may not be done in pubs, the most visible has been the legislation concerning opening hours. Although Sunday hours had been an issue, pubs opened from early in the morning until late at night up to the time of World War I. The wartime government of Lloyd George became seriously worried about drunkenness, especially among munitions workers. 'We are fighting Germany, Austria and drink,' said the Prime Minister, 'and the greatest of these deadly foes is drink.' Laws introduced then, and formalized after the war, were the basis of opening hours which have inconvenienced civilized man ever since. Hours in different towns have been made more consistent over the years, but there is still ample opportunity for confusion even among seasoned pub-goers. In cities, pubs usually open from 11.0 in the morning to 3.0 in the afternoon, and from 5.0 or 5.30 in the evening to 11.0 at night, though those in non-residential business districts may exercise their freedom to close in mid-evening and at weekends.

Alive and well . . . village life. Fête outside the Tucker's Arms at Dalwood, near Axminster, Devon.

Country times are usually half an hour earlier, though certain pubs may stay open longer on market days. When London's wholesale fruit and vegetable market was in Covent Garden, late revellers in the West End used to take advantage of the pubs that opened at 5.0 in the morning for porters. In order to pose as a *bona fide* porter it was often necessary to down a glass of whisky with hot milk. Similarly, a fast and considerable capacity for strong ale is required in any pub which may open at odd hours for miners or other shift-workers.

The incursion of 30,000 hard-drinking industrial workers into the rural Scottish border area to man a massive explosives factory led to another significant measure during World War I. Breweries and pubs in the area were placed under State control. State management also opened its own pubs, with a minimum of interior advertising (no mirrors or brewer's signs) and the maximum of distractions from drink (newspaper racks, billiards, bowling greens and the like). Those were the only pubs ever conceived with the purpose of discouraging drinking, but they came to be well-liked. The state-brewed beer, produced on the English side of the border, in Carlisle, enjoyed a particularly good reputation among drinkers. Although a much smaller scheme at Enfield, near London, was scrapped after the war, Carlisle's State beer and 170 State pubs survived until the Conservative Government of 1970 denationalized them.

In *The Beer Drinker's Companion*, Frank Baillie comments: 'After half a century of excellent service to Carlisle and district, the State Management Scheme is being wound up. After World War I, when it was no longer needed, it was continued. Now, when it has become accepted, it is to be ended – apparently against the wishes of the local people. Not a very good example of democracy at work.'

At the time, people all over England were complaining about the effects of 'rationalization' being carried out by the big brewers. A book entitled *The Death of the English Pub* was written by Christopher Hutt, though such polemics were to help ensure that the fatality had been exaggerated.

When the 200-year-old *White Horse* in Sutton, near Petworth, Sussex, was declared uneconomic by the national company Allied Breweries, the villagers faced a future without a pub. The *White Horse* was bought for £26,500 by an individual, author Ian Anstruther, who explained his expensive gesture by saying: 'I have spent the money in defence of principle – villages like this should not be allowed to die. Sutton was becoming like a lot of other villages in the area – just a street of houses. If the pub had gone, it would have been a complete end to village life.'

Hilaire Belloc thought that more than the village was at stake: 'When you have lost your inns, drown your empty selves, for you will have lost the last of England.'

Sign Language

A history in the streets

ALE-STAKE and traditional painted signboard. The latter style is enjoying a colourful revival after a period in which national brewers often substituted their own logotypes for the illustrations. The grand Victorian variation is at Salford, Greater Manchester. The house's name probably originates from the practice of erecting pubs to billet construction workers during bridge-engineering (as happened in the case of church-building). 'Vault' is a Lancashire equivalent of 'public bar.' Elsewhere in the North, the plural 'Vaults' is more common, or 'tap-room.'

AN ENDLESS PUB-CRAWL would afford the best lesson in England's heritage and history. What other country has painted its story in the streets, hung the pictures at every corner, every roadside and village, like a continuous tapestry, and captioned them with wit, rhyme and comment? From the ubiquitous *Green Man* (pre-Christian) to the unique *Dog and Trumpet* (1970s), England's every square mile is a vast, open-air museum, detailing its own geography, topography, military history, heraldry; its personalities, birds and beasts, occupations and sports.

Other lands have names for their bars or cafés, but not quite like the English names. Other lands have tavern-signs of a kind, but the English variety is unique in its extent and range, its imagination and colour. So much so that English pub names have evolved an idiom of their own. When the comedian Ted Ray used to mention the *Frog and Nightgown* in his radio show, did any listener need to be told that he was talking about a pub (there is at least one such house, in London's Old Kent Road)? Which visitor to England has not looked out for the *Pig and Whistle* (a name which is used by only a dozen or so pubs, contrary to popular myth)?

England has had inn-signs of a sort since the occupying Romans hung vine-bushes outside the *tavernae* where their soldiers could buy wine. This practice, from which originates the saying, 'a good wine needs no bush,' may have been introduced to England even earlier. The Phoenicians, who used much the same device, are said to have landed in the far West Country for the purpose of trade. As early as 1393, King Richard II had made compulsory something similar, which he called the 'ale-stake,' so that his tasters could monitor all establishments selling drink and ensure that it was being brewed to an adequate standard. Thus ale-house keepers became the first tradesmen compelled by law to display a sign.

Vine-bushes, ale-stakes, and other simple indications of the

AN EXOTIC sign which is not uncommon in rural England. The Saracen's Head, at Newton Green, near Sudbury, Suffolk. (Tolly Cobbold is one of the county's beers.) Another Saracen's Head, at Beaconsfield, Buckinghamshire, featured in the writings of G. K. Chesterton. The Saracen was depicted in the stories of returning Crusaders as a fierce giant, whom they had shown great courage in fighting. Another, unique, sign originating from the Crusades, is the Trip to Jerusalem, in Nottingham (facing page).

wine-shop or brewhouse are remembered in some of today's popular pub-names. The *Bunch of Grapes* is a good example, and there is a well-known house of that name in Knightsbridge, London. The *Jolly Brewer, Jolly Maltster* and *Malt Shovel* speak for themselves. The *Three Tuns* were the arms of the vintners – a tun is a cask formerly used as a measure for wine or beer. Later, pubs were named after other occupations: sometimes because the ale-house keeper had another job, and let his wife look after the place; sometimes because a certain trade was practised in the area. Hence the *Baker's* or *Blacksmith's*, the *Spinner's* or *Watermen's*.

As carved and painted signs emerged, it was natural in a time of illiteracy that heraldic symbols should be used by inn-keepers to announce their business. Because so many of the early inns were run by abbeys and priories, simple ecclesiastical themes were used. Typical were the *Noah's Ark* or *Good Samaritan*.

Perhaps the most basic motif of all, the *Adam and Eve*, was in 1515 adopted by the trade body of the London Fruiterers. Clearly this was not taken to mean that they were selling forbidden fruit, for the sign became particularly popular in orchard areas. The most appropriately-named pub in England must be the *Adam and Eve*, in the village of Paradise, Gloucestershire.

In Nottingham, the *Trip to Jerusalem* is one of the several claimants to the title of England's oldest inn. Set into the rock on which Nottingham Castle stands, the inn is said to have been the assembly point for an advance party of the Second Crusade, in 1189. The Crusades were also the origin of the many *Saracen's Head* inns and probably most of the *Turk's Head* signs. Returning Crusaders are believed to have brought back the first Jerusalem *Artichoke*, providing a novel name for a pub in Christow, Devon.

The *Mitre* is one ecclesiastical sign which survived the

THE MOST LAVISH SIGN EVER . . . A GILDED 'GALLOWS'

THE MOST elaborate of signs was at Scole, in Norfolk. In 1655, it cost a then-staggering £1,000 to build. Among similar signs which still survive is the less-extravagant example on the right, at Stamford, Lincolnshire. One such sign collapsed in Fleet Street, London, killing two people and ripping apart the pub which it advertised. But two royal edicts failed to stop the building of carved and gilded 'gallows.'

Reformation intact, because Protestant bishops continued to wear the same headgear. The *Cross Keys*, originally intended to depict the symbol of St Peter, looked sufficiently secular to escape the urgent attention of zealous Protestants. But the Reformation and the later Puritan era did bring about a whole series of fascinating changes in England's inn-signs.

St Paul's description of hope as 'the anchor of the soul, secure and steadfast' inspired several variations of this theme. *We Anchor in Hope* may have been abbreviated to become the *Anchor* after the Reformation and subsequently embellished to become the *Crown and Anchor*, assuming an appropriately Naval significance with England's growth as a maritime power.

The *Salutation*, showing the Archangel Gabriel greeting the Virgin Mary, was a popular sign which was hastily toned-down after the Reformation. In some cases, it was thought sufficient to liquidate the Virgin Mary, regarded as the most Popish element, and let the inn remain as the *Angel*. In other cases, the two figures were re-styled as the *Soldier and Citizen*. Or merely the hands were left, so that the original greeting became the *Hand in Hand*. Equally, the *Hand and Flower* was a way of retaining the lily, symbol of the Virgin's purity, within a secular image. This sign might eventually become the *Lily*, or the *Flower Pot*, and the refurbishing of signs over the years has often removed all traces or suggestion of the original significance.

The *Angel* in Grantham, Lincolnshire, only became the *Angel and Royal* after a visit by Edward VII, despite its earlier

AT THE SIGN OF THE FIG LEAF . . .

FORBIDDEN: When the brewers rejected the painting of Adam and Eve intended for a pub sign at the village of Braughing, near Hertford, the artist amended it by adding a fig-leaf. This time, there were objections among the local community, so the artist started again, in a more 'classical' vein.

Detail of 'figleaf' left.

KEEPING the faith: Unusual examples of signs which retained their ecclesiastical symbolism. The Cross Keys still hangs at Rode, in Somerset. The Hope and Anchor pub, at Tottenham, London, closed in 1970. The most overtly ecclesiastical, the Olde Cross, is at Alnwick, historic county town of Northumberland. Despite its piety, the pub has an interesting curse among its attractions.

links with several monarchs. Other pubs would later acquire this type of double-barrelled name when two houses with different names merged their business, or two licences were combined. A more natural combination, the *St George and Dragon*, was often de-canonized after the Reformation, and sometimes lost the fiery beast whose defeat the sainthood celebrated. In later years, the *George* would seem suitably loyal to several of England's kings. The *Pope's Head*, then a popular sign, was naturally replaced, by order of Henry VIII, with the *King's Head*.

One notable *Pope's Head* existed in later years in the City of London, though its name may have been established in the reign of the pro-Catholic Charles II. The inn, patronized by Pepys, was demolished in 1828, but its name lives on in Pope's Head Alley.

There are more than 400 *King's Heads* in England, 300 *Queen's Heads* and 1,000 *Crowns*, making the latter by far the most popular emblem under which to drink. Some inns, rather than

SKILFUL and uncommon: Artists are often commissioned to produce just one sign, but several brewers employ regular painters. Working on the heraldic sign in the top picture is Mervyn Bown, who paints for the Devenish breweries, in the West of England. Stanley Chew, who also works in the West, has made a rich and colourful contribution to the region's pubs, illustrating many of Bass Charrington's signs.

PRECEDING PAGE: Sign on glass, at the Sawyer's Arms, Deansgate, Manchester.

being named the *King's Head*, preferred to be the *King's Arms* – referring, of course, not to his limbs, but to his coat of arms. Many of these houses have signs bearing the crest of a particular monarch, thus adding personality to what may be an otherwise undistinguished pub.

Having established that it was a sign of patriotism and upright citizenship to hang the king above what might well turn out to be the scene of drunken and loutish behaviour, the English pursued the idea with enthusiasm. The legendary chief of the ancient Britons, *King Lud*, is remembered in two London inns close to each other on Ludgate Hill, not far from St Paul's Cathedral.

The only monarch ever to object to being depicted on an inn sign was Elizabeth I, and her concern was the manner in which she was shown. Forever sensitive about her appearance, she commissioned an official portrait in 1563 for use outside taverns, and issued a Royal proclamation that all others, 'by unskilful and common paynters,' be 'knocked in pieces and cast into the fire.' The present Elizabeth's portrait, usually based on the well-known Annigoni painting, has replaced her namesake's on several boards, but the Virgin Queen remains second only to Victoria in numerical popularity.

Victoria wasn't always popular, but many signs were erected in her honour after the celebrations for her jubilee in 1887, an event which boosted business in every pub in the country. The *Jubilee* was also commemorated in the names of pubs built at the time, like the solidly-comfortable house opposite the Town Hall in Leeds, Yorkshire, well decked in red plush, cut-glass and brasswork. Several members of Victoria's family were popular topers, and her uncles George IV and William IV have their share of signs.

In the days when Britain was a great power, rattling her sabre against those of other nations, allies were toasted in tap-rooms, then denigrated when foreign policy changed. Oliver Goldsmith noted: 'An ale-house keeper near Islington, who had long lived at the sign of the French King, upon the commencement of the last war pulled down his old sign and put up that of the *Queen of Hungary*. Under the influence of her red face and golden sceptre, he continued to sell ale till she was no longer the favourite of his customers; he changed her, therefore, for the *King of Prussia*, who may be changed in turn for the next great man that shall be set up for vulgar admiration.'

The doctoring of inn-signs had been a persistent habit. Before the battle of Bosworth Field, Richard III stayed at one of the many inns which displayed as their sign his *White Boar* crest. As a guest of such honour, he was served by the landlord personally. Next day, when Richard lay dead, his body not yet cold, the landlord was busy with a pot of paint. The *Blue Boar* was, conveniently, the Earl of Oxford's crest . . . and he had been on

THE ROYAL FAMILY

WHITBREAD

H VI

KING'S HEAD

HENRY VII

Bass Charrington

King's Head

VICTORIA QUEEN HOTEL

King's Head

A.D. 1389

BLACKBOYS INN

HARVEY & SON (LEWES) LTD

WITH MORE than 400 King's Heads, and at least 300 Queen's Heads, monarchs are by far the most popular symbols in alcoholic heraldry. There are any number of Henrys (top: the Sixth, Seventh and Eighth), but the last of them gained the edge by taking over from the Pope. Victoria is the most popular Queen, with many of her signs clearly dating from the period after her jubilee in 1887. Inns did not dare hang Charles I once he had been be-headed, but his nickname, 'The Black-boy,' was a substitute. Inn-keepers who were challenged over this sign could swear it referred to a Moorish boy.

37

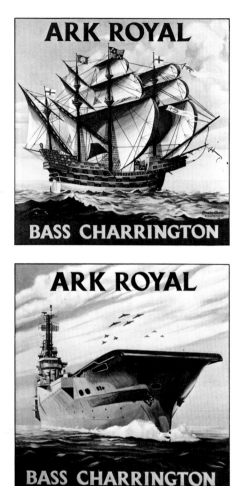

HEROICS: Ark Royals of two periods in England's great naval history sail back-to-back on a sign in the maritime city of Plymouth. An inventive example of the sign-painter's art, executed in Devon by Stanley Chew. Lord Clyde (facing page) is enshrined in the decorative tiling of the Victorian period, though his pastoral setting has suffered over the years from its location in the city-centre of an industrial metropolis. The Lord Clyde is in Deansgate, amid the Victoriana of Manchester.

the winning side. Likewise the *White Rose* of York often turned red, becoming the Lancastrian symbol, after their 30-year war (the *Rose and Crown* has a red flower, because it commemorates the victorious Henry's accession to the Throne).

Victors were not always celebrated with such cynicism. Almost every town has a pub named after *Admiral Nelson*, his ship the *Victory*, or his triumph at the battle of *Trafalgar*. Not far from his birthplace, at Burnham Overy Staithe, in Norfolk, Nelson's portrait is the sign of a pub called the *Hero*. In 1963, the brewers who owned the pub decided that Nelson should be replaced by Guy Gibson, v.c., who led the Dambusters' bomber squadron in the Second World War. The brewers had unthinkingly forgotten local pride, and the subsequent outcry ensured that Nelson won another battle more than 150 years after his death.

Nelson's contemporary the *Duke of Wellington* has about 400 pubs in his name, including one at Hastings, Sussex, which once served as his headquarters. After World War II, this pub's name was shortened to become the *Wellington*, and illustrated with a painting of the famous bomber. This time there was no objection, perhaps because the bomber itself was named after the Duke.

The English do not accept heroism uncritically. When Lord Cardigan led 600 men of the Light Brigade into a fatal charge against a battery of Russian guns, the heroism of his action was questioned in some quarters. So was a suggestion that two taverns on his land at Morley, Yorkshire, should be re-named in his honour. Yorkshiremen never were easily led. A local woollen manufacturer said the decision to re-name the pubs 'was arbitrary and needless,' and each pub has been known as *The Needless* ever since.

The people's struggle is inexorable. A band of Kentish men marched behind Wat Tyler in the Peasants' Revolt of 1381, an early upsurge of the proletariat which has a justly remembered place in English history. Tyler was killed by the Lord Mayor of London, and the rebels returned in disarray to their meeting place, the *Rose and Crown*, in Dartford. Ever afterwards, the pub was known as *Wat Tyler's*, but it was more than 500 years before the brewery which owned the pub officially recognized the name. In radical-chic Hampstead, Tyler's closest comrade has long been remembered in *Jack Straw's Castle*, said to be on the site of his last stand.

Less romantic issues have demonstrated communities' feelings over the names of their pubs. Near Dartford, at Lydd, the owning brewery suggested that a more appropriate name should be found for the *Railway* pub after the local branch-line was closed. A competition was organized to establish what should be the pub's new name. The locals refused to stretch their minds on behalf of the brewery; if they couldn't have the *Railway*, they decreed, they would call the pub the *Station*. And they did.

When a brewery wanted to follow the bandwagon of the

musical *Camelot* by attaching its name to a pub, they foolishly chose a house in Bearsted, Kent, that was named after the county's emblem, the *White Horse*. The new sign went up, but everyone still calls the pub the *White Horse*. On the other hand, there were no objections when the forgettably-named *New Inn*, near Fairlawne racing stables, in Shipbourne, Kent, was named the *Chaser* in honour of a popular local trainer.

The most successful changes of name are those bestowed by the regular customers, who know and love their pubs. Two Soho houses are classic examples of this – and that tiny village in the centre of London offers a splendid range of pub-names, all within a few minutes' walk of each other.

Some of Soho's pubs are as cosmopolitan as the village itself has been for years; others are as English as its origins. It was a Dutchman called De Hem who inspired regulars to re-name the Macclesfield pub. He was the licensee of the pub, in Macclesfield

THREE-DIMENSIONAL signs add a dramatic touch to pub buildings all over England. Many a giant feline stands silhouetted on the roof of a house called the Black Lion or White Lion, and here a golden beast graces a hostelry in Weymouth, Dorset. Other animals, like horses, deer, bears, eagles, swans and ravens feature in the elevated zoo – and so do humans such as the witch-like Old Mother Shipton. In her charac-teristic pointed hat, the Yorkshire seer contemplates the town of Portsmouth, far from her native Knaresborough.

Street, and he made it famous for both its beer and its seafood. The poet Swinburne used to travel ten miles a day during the oyster season to eat at the *Macclesfield's* long marble bar, and he wrote some verses which were hung there: 'When oysters to September yield, And grace the grotto'd Macclesfield, I will be there, my dear De Hem, To wish you well and sample them.' The brewers ripped out the grotto'd interior in 1968, and the oysters went, too. But the revamped pub's new sign is honest enough about its glorious past. It reads, *De Hems*.

While Swinburne trekked to *De Hems*, three generations of writers and artists have been equally proprietorial about another Soho pub, just across Shaftsbury Avenue, in Dean Street. Augustus John, Dylan Thomas, Malcolm Lowry, Brendan Behan and Francis Bacon have all patronized the *York Minster*, though none of them ever called it that. Few people in Soho would even recognize the name *York Minster* at first mention. The pub is said

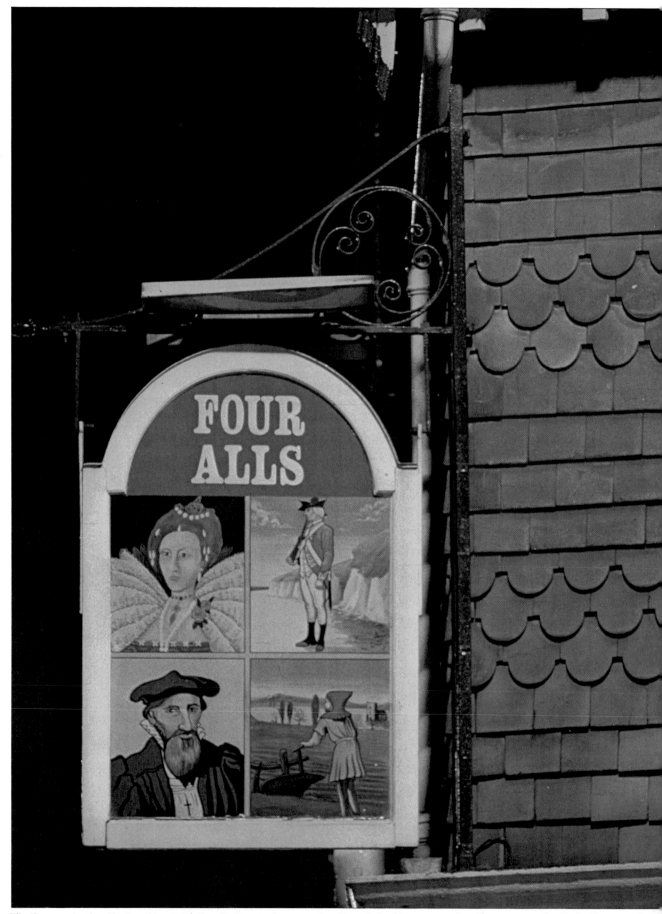

The Queen rules for all, the soldier fights for all, the preacher prays for all, and the farmer grows for all . . . country homily in Taunton, Some

to have ecclesiastical connections, and the barrel-shaped clock of the bomb-scarred St Anne's Church opposite is rumoured to have been made from two large tuns belonging to the *York Minster*, but its fame dates from the day it was taken over by Victor Berlemont. This landlord was French, and he turned the pub into a corner of Paris: Pernod, pewter water-cooler and all. General de Gaulle, exiled in London during the Second World War, met his compatriots there. The *York Minster* is only ever known by one name: the *French Pub*.

The *Swiss Tavern*, the *Helvetia*, and the *Sun and Thirteen Cantons* represent another national group among Soho immigrants. The Swiss came to Soho 200 years ago; despite all their pubs, they are now less evident in person than the Italians and the Chinese. A little further colour is added by the *Pillars of Hercules*, a Greek way of looking at the Straits of Gibraltar, and the *Golden Lion of England* is a reminder that Soho's soil is British.

Soho and the immediately neighbouring parts of London have so many *Blue Posts* that one, a pub particularly popular for its good beer, changed its name in 1975 to avoid endless confusion. Taking advantage of a pub closure somewhere else, the landlord of the *Blue Posts* in Kingly Street eagerly snapped up a redundant sign depicting *Charles II*. The sign is attractive enough, but it is has none of the significance of the old one, which accompanied the words *Blue Posts* with a hunting scene, the relevance of which may not have been immediately clear. When the bustling area now called Soho was open country, it was used for hunting. The word Soho was a hunting cry, the opposite of Tallyho, and *Blue Posts* marked the boundaries of the sporting lands.

This would also seem to explain the *Intrepid Fox*, in Wardour Street, but it doesn't. The pub was once kept by a fervent supporter of Charles James Fox, who would presumably be warmed by the degree of Anglo-American co-operation that now goes on in the neighbourhood; the *Intrepid Fox* is the local pub of the British film industry, handily placed for the cutting rooms and colour labs of Wardour and Dean Streets.

Soho has several other pubs that evoke England's green and pleasant land: two called the *Coach and Horses*, one *White Horse* and a *Green Man*. The latter was originally a pagan symbol fashioned from oak leaves, though the name was later associated with Robin Hood's Lincoln Green attire, and with a 'wild man' character in Elizabethan pageantry.

John Snow sounds like a mythical character, but wasn't. He was a surgeon whose dedicated research helped Soho beat a cholera epidemic in the early 1800s. The pub named after him stands by the site of the village water pump, which he was eventually able to declare 'safe.' The pump is said to re-appear outside the pub from time to time – an offbeat ghost.

The *Coffee House*, in Beak Street, is a typical enough pub, but

THE STREET-CRIES OF LONDON . . . CARVED IN STONE

First dimension: Some of the early pub-signs were three-dimensional designs, with considerable style and impact. These examples, now held by the Museum of London, all come from the period after the Great Fire (1666) when London was rebuilt. The Three Kings (1) was in Bucklersbury, near the Bank of England; the Bull and Mouth (2) in Aldersgate; the Three Crowns (3) Lambeth Hill; the Ape and Apple (4) in Philip Lane, near St Paul's, as was the Goose and Gridiron (5); the Boar's Head (6), in Eastcheap; and the Leather Bottle (7) in Holborn.

1

2

4

5

6

its name describes its earlier incarnation, in the 1700s. The *Cumberland Stores*, also in Beak Street, was probably a liquor 'store' – a fancy name for gin-palace – though it later became known as *Brady's* after its Irish landlord. Another of Soho's old names was abandoned in the 1970s, and replaced with surprising success. The *Marlborough*, at the entrance to Carnaby Street, where the Sixties swung, was re-named in remembrance of the period's pop music. Recalling the famous trademark of 'His Master's Voice' records, the pub is now called the *Dog and Trumpet*, an allusive name with a perfectly traditional resonance.

The *Mortal Man*, in the Lake District, was once the haunt of Wordsworth, Coleridge, Southey and De Quincy, and it is said that one of them wrote the lines which gave the pub its name: 'Oh, mortal man that lives by bread, What is it makes thy nose so red? Though silly fool that look'st so pale, Tis drinking Sally Birkett's ale.' The *Four Alls*, or sometimes *Five Alls*, probably had its origins in the fact that cobblers, with their awls, once drank there. The signs on such pubs give a more picturesque explanation, showing four figures, and the legend: 'The soldier fights for all, the farmer pays for all, the parson prays for all, and the king rules for all.' There are many variations on this theme, and the fifth figure is very likely to be the devil, who 'takes all.'

3

7

THE MUSIC goes round and round: The pub begat the music-hall, and the music-hall begat a song called 'Down at the Old Bull and Bush,' and from such proletarian origins came an upbeat reputation for the pub of that name in middle-class Hampstead. Once, the pub was noted for its neo-Georgian style, but that reputation has gone for a song.

The *Pig and Whistle* may simply originate from some obscure joke, though a fanciful explanation enjoys some currency: that it is a corruption of the Peg and Wassail, the former being the Saxons' measured drinking horn, and the latter being a word for ribald merrymaking. Likewise, it is argued that the *Goat and Compasses* is derived from the *God Encompasseth Us*; the *Cat and Fiddle* from *Catherine Fidelis*.

The most vulgar name must have been the *Flying Pisspot*, a long-gone London pub. It has a present day rival in the name which regulars have given to the *Flask*, at Hampstead. They call it the *Pig's Arse* after a rather clumsy bucolic painting in the bar.

The most cumbersome name was *The Thirteenth Mounted Cheshire Rifleman Inn*, at Stalybridge, near Manchester, until it was half-heartedly made more wieldy by the removal of the soldier from his horse. Now that he is no longer 'Mounted,' the longest pub name is *The London, Chatham and Dover Railway Tavern*.

The most dismissive name is that of a pub in Devon, at Duddiscombleigh, where the landlord in the 17th century was a solitary drinker who used to rebuff customers by shouting that there was nobody in. The pub was eventually named the *Nobody Inn*.

Drinking Styles

The mystique of English beer

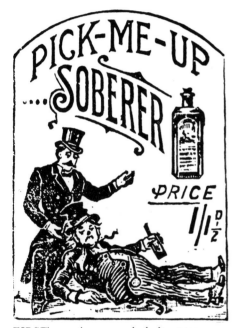

FIRST a cautionary word: don't get too drunk. 'The Greatest Remedy on Earth for Intoxication' is no longer available. This product was said to render sober a drunken person 'in about a quarter of an hour.' It was advertised by the Pick-Me-Up Company, of Leeds, in the 'Licensed Victualler's Gazette' of May 19, 1899. The more recent drinker on the left is well able to cope, as befits a durable countryman. Professional rabbit-catcher Stanley Creeper tackles a pint at his local, the Rising Sun, on haunted Bodmin Moor, in Cornwall.

GIN WOULD have done better to have stayed in Holland, where it comes from. There, it tastes more honest, adds flavour to chasers of lightweight Dutch beer, sharpens the palate for a salted herring, and keeps out the prevalent damp. Uncertain English drinkers called it 'London' or 'Plymouth' gin, as those cities would have it, but they still drown it in tonic-water – and might as well dab the scenty stuff behind the ears. Gin in pubs is an affectation. Gin is for the cocktail hour, as an aperitif (if you can't get Polish or Russian vodka), just as wine and brandy are for drinking during and after dinner.

Whisky belongs to Scotland, unless it is spelled with a penultimate 'e,' which makes it Irish. Whisky without an 'e' should be enjoyed in the Scottish Highlands or Islands, perhaps on Speyside or the Western Isles, before or after a walk in the mountain heather and a dinner of well-hung game. In Scotland, the standard measures are less mean; the 'single-malts' more plentiful; the tastes an endless variety, from silk-smooth to peat-rough, with a guaranteed afterglow. Whiskey with an 'e' is as warm as an Irish welcome, and shouldn't be drunk without one, preferably as the sun soaks through the mist on its way to meet the morning. The English have been drinking whiskies in any quantity for little more than a century, and have never really come to grips with them. Had they taken this Celtic beverage more seriously, they would never have allowed Irish to be so totally vanquished from popularity by Scotch within a decade or so of its arrival in England; if a drink is to be enjoyed, it must be allowed to express its full range of moods.

Spirits are a decoration in pubs, a diversion. The Northerners are straightforward enough about this. Ask for a Scotch in Newcastle-upon-Tyne and you'll likely get a Scotch ale. London pubs would be better places if they left spirits to the occasional houses which specialize in them. Even Chelsea's *Admiral Codrington*, in Mossop Street, and the *Turk's Head*, in Motcomb Street, Knightsbridge, could not find enough discerning customers in their wealthy hinterlands to justify each keeping about a hundred brands of Scotch. Both houses cut their range to a dozen or so.

Spirits are apt to make people drunk too speedily. Dr Johnson said: 'He who aspires to be a hero must drink brandy . . . brandy will do soonest for a man what drinking *can* do for him' (Boswell's italics). Beer works more slowly. A pint of beer takes time to swallow. The first doesn't, but the rest should.

Beer is the drink for the pub-goer. Beer drawn from a cask and served by the pint. The pint is derived from an ancient measure used for corn, and pint glasses have to be stamped to indicate the approval of the Weights and Measures Department. Time has proved that the pint is just the right quantity to tickle the palate for an expectant moment, rush headlong at the thirst, and demand a courteous amount of time for drinking before the next round falls due. People who drink half-pints are apt to grasp the beer-glass awkwardly, with their little finger sticking out. Anyone who adopts this sort of effete mannerism might be expected to be a half-pint person. Beer-drinking is a robust activity, and fancy behaviour is not encouraged.

English beer is different. Unique. There are two kinds of beer in the world: the English kind, and the kind everyone else drinks. They are quite separate brews. English beer is more robust: A tall, dark stranger of a beer, with its pint glass. In other lands, beer too often glisters like gimcrack gold, all bright and

SPIRITS are evident at every English pub, but they are still essentially foreign. Rum was imported from the West Indies; gin was Dutch until London and Plymouth adopted it; the whisky imported from North of the Border would be 'Scottish' if the English hadn't corrupted it; and the Irish spell their whiskey with a penultimate 'e' . . . but the English never did care much for the conventions of their neighbours. The drinks are on the windows in a particularly well-decorated example of the mock-antique Late Victorian pub, the Air Balloon, in Portsmouth.

300 MILES
FOR A
GLASS OF BRITISH LAGER.

Three hundred miles for a glass of Lager beer. It sounds absurd when you can go round to the corner house and get a glass of bitter. Nevertheless a number of experts on beer went three hundred miles instead of going round the corner.

To put it plainly, Messrs. Samuel Allsopp and Co. organised on Wednesday last an excursion—a most delightful excursion—to Burton-on-Trent, in order to show to the United Kingdom and to the World that the great little town in the valley of the Trent is worthy of its fame, and equal to the production of beer in all its stages of superiority of quality—competent to compete with Continental rivals.

It wasn't so much the thirst that affected us early on the morn of the 17th instant, as the invitation from the directors of Messrs. Allsopp and Co., Limited, to catch a train leaving Euston at 9.55 that made us search our wardrobe for waterproofs, mufflers, thick boots, and rugs. It looked like being an awful day.

Regardless of consequences we ran the gauntlet of chill and fog that holds us with a damp and uncomfortable wreath, so much identified with London in October, and cabbed it to Euston. All was damp until we entered the "special" provided for us to taste this one glass of Lager beer—the first that has ever been produced in the British Isles. A glass of Lager, perhaps, might never be very magnetic, because the very name spells Continental. But the fact that we were offered the glass from Burton-on-the-Tr̶e̶

Metropolis ~~~~~~ made us plunge thro~~

from the necks of bottles. There was no fog then, only | tion of the Pfaudler Vacuum system of ferment~
~~~~ dinting o~ ~sere a~ ~ellow "leaves~ ~~ are perfectly fermented ~~~~ to six o

CONSIGNMENT OF THE PFAUDLER VACUUM COMPANY'S CYLINDERS FROM NEW YORK FOR BRITISH LAGER BEER.

STEAM BREWERY . . . the train is hauling American equipment to a brewery in the English beer-town of Burton. The report, from a turn-of-the-century edition of the 'Licensed Victuallers' Gazette,' talked about 'hands across the sea' . . . 'Yankee' plant being imported to England's 'Metropolis of Beer.' The equipment was supplied by the Pfaudler Vacuum Fermentation Company, of New York, in whose honour Allsopp's Burton brewery flew the Stars and Stripes alongside the Union Jack. The object of this Anglo-American venture was to find a cheaper way of producing Bavarian-style beer in England. Although Allsopp's enterprise extended to a facility-trip for journalists (a remarkably early use of this public-relations technique), the 'Gazette' reporter evinced a scepticism that has survived to this day. Would the English drinker ever accept this so-called lager beer when 'the very name spells Continental'?

shiny, and transparent; English beer has impenetrable depths. Other lands' beers have distinctive tastes, but few have the body and character of the English type.

English beer is an acquired taste, or a series of acquired tastes, like oysters, steak tartare, or marron glacé. Like sex, it is a pleasure which can better be appreciated with experience, in which variety is both endless and mandatory. The pleasure lies, too, in gaining the experience: the encounters with the unexpected, the possibility of either triumph or disaster, the pursuit of the elusive, the constant lessons, the bitter-sweet memories that linger. Other countries have as many beers as England has, but no country can offer such a range of distinct tastes.

The difference is more than skin-deep. The fine, upright beers of Munich and Pilsen owe their parentage to a monk who journeyed from the one town to the other in 1842 to bring the word of a new yeast he had discovered. His yeast spawned beer in Copenhagen in 1845, and later spread to Dortmund and such places. The beers of Amsterdam and Brussels, Melbourne and Milwaukee, are of the same yeast. The insular English stayed characteristically aloof. No newfangled beer for them. In the 1840s, England was in no mood to take lessons from foreigners. Other countries could use a yeast that fermented at the base of the brew, but the English would still do it at the top. Other countries could use a yeast that fermented cool, but the English would still do it at a warmer temperature.

Beer tastes best, most fully expresses its flavour, at the temperature at which it was fermented. That is why the rest of the world drinks its beer cool, while the English drink theirs warmer. What the rest of the world gains in the thirst-quenching cold edge, the English gain in a gentler, and more subtle, palate.

Rituals survive in mid-Wiltshire . . . unloading malt for the fine naturally-conditioned beers brewed by Wadworth's, of Devizes.

The Englishman abroad goes along with local beer-drinking habits. At home, foreign brews are not even accepted as beer. As if to emphasize their foreign-ness, they are called by a name that is both imprecise and German – 'lager.' When English breweries add a 'lager' to their range, they give it a Teutonic brand-name. When English drinkers buy a 'lager,' they are quite likely to sugar the pill by adding lime – an insult which no beer, however foreign, deserves. 'Lager' was introduced to Wales in 1882, and became common in Scotland before making much impression in England. Despite its increasing acceptance, it remains a separate drink from beer in the Englishman's mind, and has little more than 15 per cent of the whole British market. The popular understanding is that 'lager' beers have a certain novelty value, and are suitable for women and hot days.

English beer was haughty enough in the 19th century, but it nearly died in the 20th. The traumatic period was the 1960s, when the traditional drink was assaulted and oppressed almost to vanishing point by marketing men, accountants and economists, during a wave of brewery takeovers. Then, in the early 1970s, came a widespread grass-roots revival which flourished to a degree no one had expected. A new level of awareness, and a militancy, emerged among English beer-drinkers. Beer became a subject of contention in the media. Connoisseurs began to make their reputations; beer-snobs to proliferate. It was a renaissance for English beer, a boom period for certain fashionable brewers. Beer was chic.

In the 1960s, the marketing men and their friends had destroyed local breweries, and replaced their distinctive products by developing 'national brands,' often chilled, filtered, pasteurized and artificially carbonated, each of which acts damaged the beer's flavour. This trail of corporate vandalism had left beers sterile and feeble, but easy to handle.

Landlords accustomed to taking care so that beer would not be 'bruised' as the wooden barrels were loaded into their cellars, had become redundant. Because secondary fermentation no longer went on in the barrel, the careful rituals of 'soft-pegging' and 'hard-pegging,' with their critical timing, ceased to be a measure of the landlord's craft. Nor were finings, made from the sturgeon's swim-bladder, any longer added at this stage to settle the beer.

Brightly-coloured plastic devices sprouted hideously on bars, hiding the pressure-taps which had replaced the tall handles of the ebony-and-brass beer-pulls. The new brews were called 'keg' beers, though the description hardly fitted a pre-processed product delivered in a huge sealed can. Admen burned the midnight oil (or gin-and-tonic) to devise new brand-names for brews; often, the names were perfectly apposite for liquids that frothed like detergents. No copywriter described the 'national brands' with quite the colour and accuracy of the disgruntled

HIDEOUS plastic devices sprouted on bars, announcing the availability of nationally-marketed beer brands. Sometimes they imposed their vulgar company on the tall and dignified ebony-and-brass handles of the traditional beer-pulls. Even tiny breweries like Donnington (facing page) began to keg some of their beer. In other respects, the brewery is a vignette of unspoiled England: its mill-pond alive with wildfowl, many of them exotic; its waterwheel; and its owner at work on the premises, assisted by his dog. The brewery, in local stone, lies in a fold of the Cotswold hills, at Stow-in-the-Wold, Gloucestershire, close to the border with Oxfordshire. It even has its own road-sign.

drinker who said that they were, 'all piss and wind, like a barber's cat.'

The fate that had overtaken so many of life's pleasures seemed set to overtake beer, and to do so irreversibly. The distinctive was being wiped out by the bland. A new generation of drinkers was growing up having known nothing other than 'national brands,' and suspicious of anything with taste.

Of all the 'national brands,' none offended conservationists more than Watney's 'Red Barrel.' Wherever 'Red Barrel' appeared, there was a danger that Watney's corporate policies of that particular period might follow: not only would local beers be replaced, but the pubs would be emasculated, too, with such 'old-fashioned' amenities as dart-boards and pianos being thrown out. To some drinkers, Watney's – as capitalistic a company as any – epitomized the Corporation versus the People. When their American-owned advertising agency Leo Burnett relaunched Watney's national brand, using its name in a patronizing pun – announcing a 'Red Revolution' – their sense of humour was not shared by all drinkers. It may not be coincidence that the counter-revolution, against 'national brands,' began to gain ground at almost the same time as the 'Red' launch, with the establishment of the Campaign for Real Ale.

The Dunkirk Spirit, a necessary precondition to any energetic action on the part of the English people, could be invoked once it was established that a national institution – pub life – was in danger. Friends began to exchange details of pubs with unspoiled beer in a spirit of conspiracy, as if they were part of some resistance movement, which in their way they were. A handful of houses, like the *Barley Mow*, near the historic city of St Albans, began to specialize in beer – the very product which had once been every pub's stock-in-trade. Pubs such as the *Barley Mow* became almost beer museums. One of the scruffiest pubs in England, *Becky's Dive*, near London Bridge railway station, suddenly became the destination for an interminable stream of beer-fanciers, anxious to sample its astonishing selection of brews.

The *Good Beer Guide*, a cheap paperback produced by the Campaign for Real Ale, had sold out within days of its second full-scale edition hitting the bookstalls in 1975. The Campaign bought its own pub, the *Nag's Head*, in Hampstead, and houses in Cambridge, Bristol, Leeds, and other cities.

At first, the drink conglomerates were able to dismiss the Campaign for Real Ale without even bothering to disguise their contempt, but before long the brewers were competing with each other either to promote forgotten brands or to reintroduce in some pubs beers which were more acceptable to this 'minority of cranks.' It will take time to gauge the long-term future of traditional English beers, but the mid-1970s will be remembered as one of those occasions when the customer fought back. One of Europe's most successful consumer campaigns had been born.

'Real ale' has been compared with health-foods, an analogy which bodes badly for its retail price (until mass-marketing reached its crisis of resistance, the 'national brands' had been the more expensive, despite often being weaker than the 'real ales'). A better comparison would set bread baked in a local shop against mass-marketed pap. 'National brands' are the worst thing since sliced bread. Like most mass-marketed breads, they are produced to keep for a long time with a minimum of care; they are intended to offer brewers economies of scale, although this has not always worked out; they are necessary to the convenient advertising of beer on network television; but, above all, they are intended to expand the brewers' constituency by attracting women and inexperienced drinkers. 'National brands' lack subtlety of flavour, palate, bouquet. They are also a great deal sweeter than many of the traditional beers – not in itself a complaint until the original beers are either taken off the market,

THE TRADITIONAL WAY TO PULL A PINT

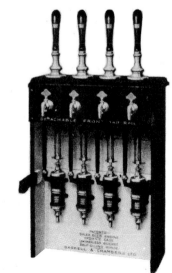

HAND-PULLS, sometimes painted, should indicate a good pint. (Above and right, Buller's pottery). That is unless they are 'fakes,' left to mislead the drinker. Beer was drawn straight from the cask until the 'beer-engine' was devised in 1797. The new method meant that beer could be pumped from a cool cellar when necessary. This simple suction system does not impair the natural condition of beer, but many drinkers are less happy about more modern methods.

or themselves rendered sweeter to meet a 'public taste' which has more to do with supply than demand.

Many of the most famous bitters taste as their name suggests they should, and a detail of English life would be obliterated if they ceased to be available, but it is equally true that a good number of respected brews have a sweet palate. There is no such thing as a definitive English beer taste. A scientist who attempted what he described as 'a sensory analysis of beer flavours' in England, in order to produce a 'standard vocabulary of tastes,' found that his respondents used more than 250 terms to describe the beers they drunk. These ranged from 'sickly,' 'toffee-like' and 'buttery' to 'nutty,' 'earthy' and 'cabbagy'. Nor is there an optimum potency, though drinkers would be glad if brewers made clearer the strength of their products.

The descriptions which the more traditionally-minded brewers apply to their bitters do nothing to minimize the con-

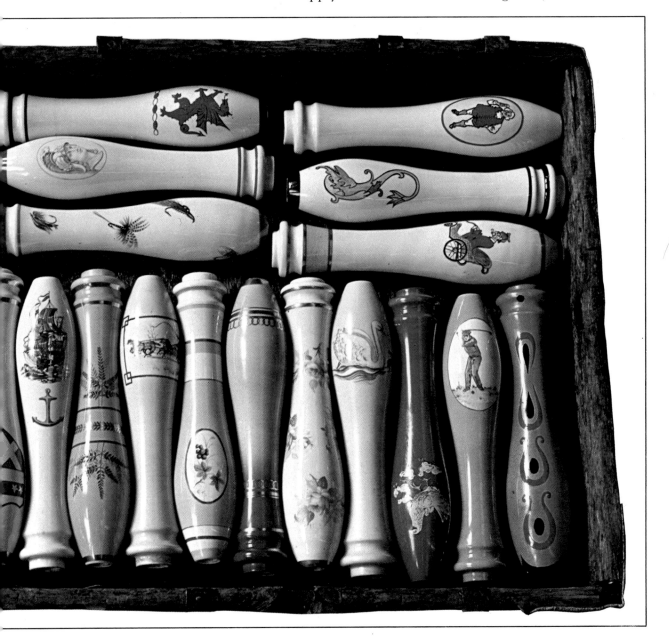

THE CHAUVINISM of beer: To some Englishmen, the word 'Newcastle' indicates a beer rather than a proud city, famous for coal, shipbuilding and football. When the region's famous brewery appends the blue-star trademark to its name, no one can be in any doubt. This example of licensed graffiti is in the local suburb of Gosforth. At the opposite end of the country, McMullen's (right) offer local malt, Mr Pudge's champion prize hops, and a product which – being indubitably British – is most certainly best. Even in those distant days, when stout was eight old pennies a pint ('Public Bar Prices'), McMullen's were anxious to point out that their beer was naturally matured, neither chilled nor artificially carbonated.

fusion. 'Special' or 'Best' bitter may not necessarily be better than the ordinary brew; it may be stronger, slightly sweeter, or have more body, but this varies from brewer to brewer. 'Light ale' or 'Pale' is just another name for bitter; if both are offered, the latter is likely to be the stronger. It doesn't usually alter any from being described as 'India Pale Ale, or 'IPA' (originally a beer brewed for the East India Company) or 'Export.' All of these names are used for draught beers, but are more commonly applied when the various bitters are bottled. Mild may become 'brown ale' in its bottled manifestation.

The famous 'Newcastle Brown Ale,' which has a mixed reputation among connoisseurs, would more properly be described as a 'Strong Ale.' It is not available on draught, and its unusual clear-glass pint bottles are instantly recognized by serious beer-drinkers. Most brewers make a 'Strong Ale', of one

degree or another, sometimes calling them 'Old Ale' or 'Barley Wine.' The latter, a fruity beer, may be matured for 18 months or more, and drunk in small glasses – 'nips' – usually during the winter.

Stout is a heavy beer made with an added proportion of roasted barley, and often well hopped. 'Milk stout' is a name which has fallen out of popular use since the Trades Descriptions Act, but it was used to describe 'sweet stout,' increasingly the preserve of old ladies. The drink got its name from the lactose which is used as a non-fermentable sugar, though the description can only have been encouraged by the coincidental presence of a dairy-farm next to the well-known Mackeson stout brewery.

'Extra' stout, the bitter and full-bodied dark beer with which the name of Arthur Guinness's brewery has become synonymous, is best drunk in Irish bars (including those in England and the United States); in pubs with lousy bitter or mild (Guinness is dependable); or on cold days. Guinness and bitter can be mixed to make a 'Black and Tan,' but the military connotations of this mixture's name are properly dangerous in the light of the recurrent Anglo-Irish Troubles. A less political permutation blends Guinness with cider, parodying the chic 'Black Velvet,' which is made from stout and champagne. People also mix draught and bottled beers to make 'light and bitter' (sometimes known as a 'light top' or a 'light split,' among other regional names) or 'brown and mild.'

Bottles, which are permitted to be of any capacity the brewer fancies, are really for taking beer home in. Bottled beer is for drinking when the pubs aren't open, or with meals. The same applies to canned beer, which is especially favoured by Australians living in Britain. Although wine is more fashionable, bottled beer is the best drink to have with English food. A good bottled bitter is a perfect accompaniment to saddle of mutton or steak-and-kidney pudding. And what could be more fitting with a curry than India Pale Ale?

Most bottled beers are matured and conditioned before they leave the brewery, though Guinness and Worthington's 'White Shield' are famous exceptions. The natural sediment thrown by fermentation in the bottle is particularly noticeable in a light-coloured bitter like 'White Shield,' and the manner in which a barman pours this renowned beer is some measure of his professional pride. Even barmen shell-shocked by hangovers have struggled manfully to maintain a gentle pouring action, thus preventing the sediment from falling into the glass. The sediment makes no difference to the taste, but offends the eye of the beer-drinker, who tends to associate a cloudy glass with a beer which has gone bad. This is a silly assumption, since some of England's finest bitters have a naturally cloudy appearance; the only criterion should be a well-schooled taste.

For all the damage wrought by the harbingers of mass-

THE RURAL SCENE is deep in the heart of urban London, at Young's brewery, in the district of Wandsworth. The ram is the company's symbol, the horses deliver beer . . . and the farmyard complements the stables. Young's is a small brewery, very popular with beer-connoisseurs, and its pubs are predominantly neighbourhood locals to the South and West of Central London.

PREVIOUS PAGE: Along with hand-pulls, wooden casks may be a sign of naturally-conditioned beer. The two often coincide, since a brewer who distributes his beers in the traditional manner may well take the same attitude towards their preparation. Some brewers – Wadworth's, in this instance – have their own coopers to make the casks. Hypercritical beermen assert that the wooden cask enhances the taste of their drink, though naturally-conditioned beers can survive equally well in the more common metal casks.

marketing, and for all the regional near-monopolies, England still has more than 70 local breweries, each producing their own half-dozen or more additions to John Barleycorn's family, numbering more than 1,000 English brands in all.

'There is a remarkable variety of draught and bottled beers up and down the country,' notes the estimable Frank Baillie, in *The Beer Drinker's Companion.* Yet, he sighs, beer-drinkers are often conservative to the point that they will barely countenance brews to which they are not accustomed. Connoisseurs of wine, he points out, do not restrict themselves in this way, drinking solely the products of their favourite chateau; nor do gourmets stick to a single variety of cheese.

Not so much conservatism as local chauvinism, dating from those distant days when every other alehouse brewed its own beer (a handful still do – see facing page). Up to the 1950s, most towns had at least one local brewery, and drinkers were aggressively partisan. They either championed the local beer to the exclusion of all others, or dismissed it because of its familiarity, in favour of an exotic import from the next town.

Legend has it that the beer-drinkers of the North and Midlands are connoisseurs. Perhaps because coal-mining, steel and other such thirst-making heavy industries are concentrated in the northern two-thirds of the country, beer consumption there is far greater than it is among the cosmopolitans of London, or the gentle folk of the South-East and West Country. The North may have deserved its reputation for strong beers when there were more to choose from, but the Midlands had a greater number of famous brands. In those days, just as the face of London is coloured by its veins of red buses, so the liveries of local brewers, painted on pub buildings in every street, made different towns instantly recognizable. Only in a town's main-street would a cluster of rivals from nearby cities make their presence known.

During the mass-marketing deluge, the geography of English beer shifted to a seismic degree. London-based drink conglomerates (one even sells milk) swallowed many of the North and Midlands' famous brews without as much as an honest English belch. Towns lost their distinctive pub-colours and their local tastes; sometimes brews were marketed under old names, but turned out to be totally new concoctions. Beer-lovers had to take to the highways and byways in search of new landmarks. Small breweries which had hitherto enjoyed no reputation began to emerge as lionized preservationists of England's alcoholic heritage. As a consequence, some small brewers experienced an increase in sales of 50 per cent in a single year, and several enjoyed a doubling of their profits in a period of three to four years.

In London, the small local brewery of Young's (not to be confused with Younger's) rightly became a favourite with beer-

THE PUBS THAT BREW THEIR OWN BEER

SOME of the best-known 'home-brew' pubs: (1) The Blue Anchor, Helston, Cornwall; (2) The Three Tuns, Bishop's Castle, Shropshire (Salop); (3) The All Nations, Madeley, Telford, Shropshire; (4) The Old Swan, Netherton, Dudley (between Birmingham and Wolverhampton). Commercial home-brewing experienced a revival in the mid-1970s. Several pubs toyed with the idea of brewing their own beer, and a number of home-brewers began to supply free-houses. Among the home-brews to achieve some reputation was that at the Miner's Arms, in Priddy, Somerset. Unfortunately, the Miner's Arms (5) is not a pub, but a restaurant, despite its name. ·

BREWING UP at the Blue Anchor. Landlord Geoffrey Richards is a third-generation home-brewer, producing a rich beer known as 'Spingo.' The pub dates back to the 15th century. It has been a monk's rest, and the scene of both murder and suicide.

buffs. Young's has only a handful of pubs in the centre of London, among which the *Guinea*, off Berkeley Square, has proved sturdy enough to cope with its considerable popularity. Many of Young's houses are utterly unpretentious London locals, in neighbourhoods on the South and West sides of town. The only other local brewery in London is Fuller's, also in the West – on the road to the airport. Fuller's 'Extra Special' is probably England's strongest draught bitter. Fuller's have a rather erratic selection of houses, one of the best of which is the historic *Dove*, on the riverside at Hammersmith.

The cities of Nottingham, Wolverhampton and Manchester are noted for their ranges of beer. Certain rural regions have a better-than-average complement of local breweries: The Thames Valley and Oxfordshire; the whole of Eastern England, from Kent to Lincolnshire, with the exception of Norfolk; the Lake District's southern and western fringes. That is not to say these regions are necessarily thick with good pubs: each local brewery may only have a scatter of houses, ranging from a dozen or so to a few hundred; sometimes all within a few miles of each other; sometimes spread over two or three counties.

The sort of brewers who win the rightful approval of connoisseurs seem to have been remarkably lucky in inheriting suitably bucolic family names: Brakspear's of Henley (noted for their picturesque pubs); Hook Norton, in Oxfordshire; Shepherd Neame, in the brewing town of Faversham; Ridley's, at Hartford End ('Draught Beer from the Wood'); Adnams' (a great favourite with connoisseurs), at Sole Bay; Bateman's (Good Honest Ales), in Lincolnshire; Ruddle's of Rutland; Marston Evershed (at Burton-on-Trent); Boddington's; Timothy Taylor's (in Yorkshire's Brontë Country); Sam Smith's (not to be confused with John Smith's, a neighbour and rival in the little brewing town of Tadcaster, near York); Theakston's; Cameron's; and Hartley's of Ulverston.

Some of these breweries have thrown themselves into the embrace of the conservationists. Adnams', for example, says of itself: 'Keg beer does not form an important part of the company's production, emphasis being on natural and traditional draught beer . . . it is felt that recent developments of mass-production can only harm the quality of the beer . . . all Adnams' beers are made from East Anglian barley, hops from Kent, Worcestershire and Herefordshire . . . references to the fine beers of Sole Bay stretch back until at least 1641 . . .'

Man has been a brewer since Mesopotamian times probably, since the discovery of wild barley, or since the ancient Egyptians unlocked the properties of yeast as an agent of fermentation, but it may be to Phoenician traders that the English owe the technique. Julius Caesar noted that the Britons made a 'high and mighty liquor,' and ale was the national drink by Christian times. The early ales, the meads and apple-ciders (still the

HOLT'S Manchester Ales in a typically unpretentious setting (facing page), the White Lion, in Eccles. Manchester is one area in which the North's reputation for fine beer remains valid. Drinkers can choose from the local brews like Holt's, Hyde's, Lees' and Boddington's, in pubs which have often escaped the worst excesses of 'interior design.'

CIDER is the traditional drink in the West of England, though the original local version is at least as rare as naturally-conditioned beers. Locals (below) at the Pike and Musket, in the small Somerset town of Street, have a tradition of wassailing the cider-apple tree on January 17. They sing an invocation that the tree will bear sacks full of apples when spring comes – and they drink home-made cider, laced with gin, from a special wassail cup.

regional drink in the West of England), the liquors that had to be flavoured with honeys and spices . . . all of these set the table for one more vital ingredient. Ale was made by coddling barley into germination, drying and browning it to a biscuity malt, infusing it in water, boiling and brewing, fermenting in storage – but it took the arrival of hops to give the drink its subtly bitter-sweet palate.

The hopped drink arrived from Continental Europe by the barrel as an import in the 15th century, and was transplanted into the soil of South-East England by Flemish settlers a hundred years later. The Flemish settlers called their drink *biere*, and it was for a time regarded as a separate beverage from the traditional ale. '*Bere* is the naturall drynke for a Dutche man,' wrote the 16th-century writer Andrew Borde. 'It is used in England to the detryment of many Englisshe people; specially it killeth them the which be troubled with the colyke, and the stone and the strangulion. For the drynke doth make a man fat, and doth inflate the bely, as it doth appere by the Dutche men's faces and belyes.' On another occasion, the eloquent Borde complained of a cloudy glass which, he said, looked as though pigs had been wrestling in it.

The 'wicked and pernicious weed hops' was at one point banned by authorities in Shrewsbury. Henry VIII's brewer was warned not to add hops or brimstone to ale. The Brewers' Company of the City of London petitioned the Lord Mayor that 'hoppes, herbs or other like things' be kept out of ale, which should be made only from 'licour (water), malt and yeste.'

Hops neatly counterpointed the insularity and the tolerance which are equally famous in the English character. Henry VI commanded the Sheriffs of the City of London in uncompromising terms: 'Certain malevolent persons, attempting out of great hatred cunningly to oppress those brewing the drink called *biere*, have sown grievous murmurings and discords so that people turn against the drink, wherefore the brewers do not dare brew the said drink of *biere*, to the damage and hardships of very many of our subjects who relish that drink and prefer to drink it as a notable, healthy and temperate drink. You shall cause it to be proclaimed that all such brewers of *biere* shall boldly make, sell and exercise as they were wont, forbidding our lieges that none of them molest or hinder those brewers of beer whereby they may not freely brew as hitherto, or use intimidation or threat to the same, under the peril that befalls.'

There are still 20,000 acres of hop 'gardens' in the South-East, mainly in Kent, and to a lesser extent in Sussex: The White Cliffs of Dover, and Hastings, to the South; the dormitory towns of London not far away. In the green and temperate West Midland counties of Herefordshire and Worcestershire, there are another 15,000 acres, known as hop 'yards.' Hop-picking in the South once provided a 'working holiday' for thousands of poor

WHITBREAD

HOP POLE

THE HOP did not easily win acceptance when it was introduced to England in the 16th century, but it grew to be a much-loved symbol, as British as the green gardens of Kent. The Hop Pole pub was, as might be expected, in that county, at East Peckham. Kent's hops yield their cones in August and September, to add the teasing bitterness and delicate aroma to England's beers. The malt is the basic ingredient, but the hop cone adds the magic. Both were a recurrent theme in early beer advertising, as evidenced by the 1932 poster on the facing page. 'AK' was one of the many sets of initials used to identify mild and bitter beers. One theory maintains that the initials in this case referred to Prime Minister Asquith (1908–16), who raised beer tax to an unprecedented level. They were said to stand for 'Asquith's Knockout.'

families from London, while people from the big industrial cities of the West Midlands did much the same in Herefordshire and Worcestershire. A hundred thousand 'imported' labourers were recorded as having worked in the South-East alone in the year 1908, and there were still 30,000 aboard 61 special trains from London Bridge station in 1945. The last lone train ran in 1960: prosperity and mechanization had together eliminated the need for such arduous 'holidays.'

The garden countryside of Kent is still given its own character by the silhouetted cowls of oast-houses, where hops are dried, though the buildings' traditional design has become less common with modernization. Some traditional oast-houses have even been converted into weekend homes for London businessmen, as if they were barns in the Dordogne. It would be hard to dispute, asserts beerman Frank Baillie, that a hop garden in summer, with its attendant oast-houses, adds a special flavour to the rural scene in this corner of the South-East.

In continental Europe, male plants are excluded from the gardens, so that hops may be seedless, as traditionally preferred by such nationalities as the Belgians, Dutch, Germans and Danes. In England, a more libertarian philosophy prevails. English beer-lovers argue that their drink will be ruined if the long arm of the European Economic Community extends itself into this area of joint agricultural policy. Maybe, but there is scant evidence as to the effect this would have on beer brewed as in England, says Baillie. Furthermore, it would be impossible to enforce such sexism, he says, because there are so many wild male hops sowing their seeds from English hedgerows.

The sensuous procedures of brewing don't die easily. The maltster who walks barefoot so as not to damage the barley on his floor, and uses wooden implements for the same reason, has not yet totally succumbed to the men in white coats who try to obtain as good results with chemical additives, and sometimes with lesser grains. The hop gardens are still busy enough, though many brewers say they get more out of the plant by converting it into an extract. Like many drinkers, Baillie has his doubts. Hop preparations may have the important acid tang, he concedes, but they seem to lack the valuable oils, resins and tannins with which the cone of the plant confers its aroma and flavour. 'Beer made with hop extract is like meat without salt.'

The wildest, the most paranoid anxieties of drinking men are exaggerated. They owe slightly less to suspicions about the ingredients of English beer than to the manner of its kegging and serving. But it is as well that Englishmen care, and increasingly voice their disquiet. The total drowning of English beer in piss and wind would be a calamity – as if French *haute cuisine* fell to the hamburger. As the 18th-century writer Sydney Smith remarked: 'What two ideas are more inseparable than beer and Britannia?'

THE FINEST MALT
THE VERY BEST HOPS
O TO MAKE
McMULLEN & SONS LTD
AK
HERTFORD
UDGE
PRIZE
AK
McMULLEN'S

The Mirror Image
The graphic art of the brewer

BY THE TIME Victorian pub-mirrors had begun to appear on the walls of apartments in London and Manhattan during the early 1970s, English brewers had realised that their mania for 'more modern' decoration was alienating customers. Some brewers started to restore mirrors and etched windows in their Victorian and Edwardian houses, and even redecorated the occasional new pub in the style of the period.

While many of the pub-mirrors sold in Carnaby Street, or advertised in the New York *Village Voice*, may have been cheap silk-screened reproductions, the brewers largely used glass decorated at considerable cost by specialist companies. The price of the craftsman's work had soared, and the insurance premiums on pub glass rocketed, but England still had a handful of merchants who could handle the work. Once, there were dozens of companies ready to decorate glass, with pubs as their main customers; for

REFLECTIONS . . . nostalgia brought out gimcrack mirrors like the one above, displayed at a shop in its home town of Newcastle-upon-Tyne. But the Real Thing had never gone away: Hundreds of pubs still have fine mirrors like the one on the left, at a pub called the Boat, in Melton Mowbray, Leicestershire. The mirror is but one manifestation of the decorative and graphic arts to be found in and around the pub.

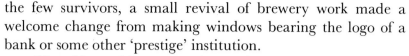

the few survivors, a small revival of brewery work made a welcome change from making windows bearing the logo of a bank or some other 'prestige' institution.

The older publicans say the work today isn't of the same quality, but the techniques are the same. The names of brewers or beers are applied on gold-leaf, often at the back of glass which is then silvered, enamelled or otherwise coated. Mirrors are sometimes tinted in pink or bronze. Coloured glass veneers can be inlaid, or ceramic paints fired into mirror-glass. Some pubs have stained-glass windows, but the most common technique is brilliant-cutting and acid etching. The brilliant-cutting is done with stones and rouges; 'French-embossing' with acid poured over masking, soda to create shading, mica to promote a stippled effect. All of these techniques, and sand-blasting, can be used to decorate a single piece of glass. The early decorative patterns for etching were derived from wrought ironwork, then the crafts-men gradually evolved their own designs, often with an elab-orate pastoral centre-piece. A whole range of tones and fibres can be acid-etched, and complemented with brilliant-cut highlights. Glass-decorators evolved their own styles of lettering, too, until their folk-art was eliminated by men in cool suits carrying corporate-design manuals.

The genre blossomed in the late Victorian period. The wealth generated by the Industrial Revolution was mak-ing its mark; the growing new middle-classes, increasingly conscious of their home surroundings, had stimulated a boom in decorative art. The bevelling of glass, brilliant-cutting, had seen considerable technical advance in the 1850s, and methods of embossing improved in the late 1880s. By the 1890s, the new electric light was widespread in pubs. Etched glass windows provided privacy, while the interior was brightly illuminated

HARDY'S CROWN (below and preceding page) was a Manchester beer which ceased to exist independently in 1962. The brewery, which operated on a local scale, was absorbed into a grouping which eventually became Bass Charrington. Hardy's name survives, weatherbeaten but colourful still, at the Albert, in Salford. The publican at the Albert, Agnes May Blyth, is pictured with a friend.
Just as brewers used windows and mirrors to advertise their products, so did distillers (facing page), though Irish whiskey began to face the challenge from Scotland in the 1870s and 1880s.

with electricity and mirrors. With many houses now owned by breweries, and whisky companies locked in combat, the opportunities for some rather sumptuous advertising were not lost. The market was growing explosively, too, with the massive increase in the population of the industrial cities.

'To the aesthetic mind, there may be nothing very beautiful in plate glass adorned with huge gilt letters setting forth the virtues of the *Dew of Ben Lomond* or the *Gatherings of Rob Roy*,' commented the *Daily News* in the late 1870s, 'but to eyes weary of

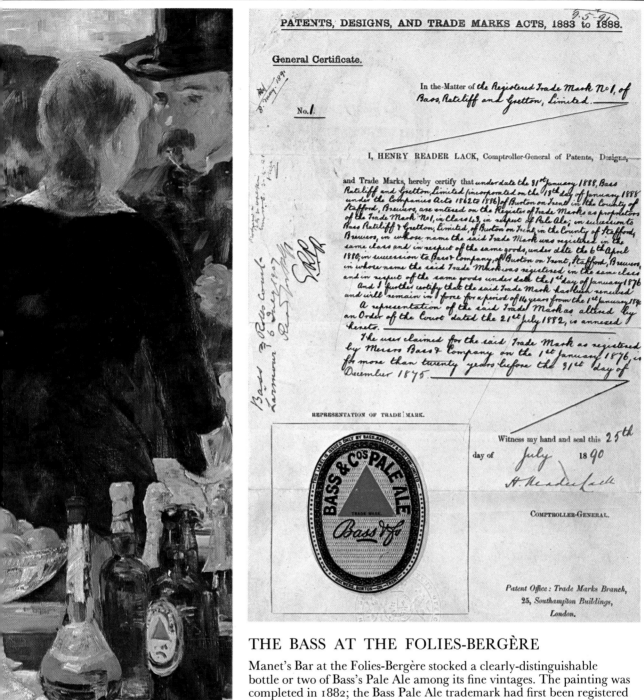

THE BASS AT THE FOLIES-BERGÈRE

Manet's Bar at the Folies-Bergère stocked a clearly-distinguishable bottle or two of Bass's Pale Ale among its fine vintages. The painting was completed in 1882; the Bass Pale Ale trademark had first been registered on January 1, 1876, as indicated by the above certificate. It was listed as Trademark Number One, a suitably eminent position for a great beer classic.

a dingy workshop, or dingier attic, these objects are more attractive than red curtains and sanded floors.' The *Daily News* had long ceased to be edited by Charles Dickens, but it clearly still maintained his concern for the life of the working man. Apart from the exotic whiskies of Ben Lomond and Rob Roy, many advertisers appeared then who are still major marketing names today. Hennessy cognac and Double Diamond beer are among those noted by Mark Girouard in *Victorian Pubs*.

Brewers and distillers, with all their competing brands and

HOW THE MODEL BREWERS DISPLAYED THEIR WARES

COLLECTORS' PIECES: Pottery toucans like this seven-inch specimen, made in 1955, were once arranged in 'flights' across pub walls. Today, they are almost extinct. This type of advertising still goes on, though Carlton Ware has given way to tougher materials. Sources dry up, too: Flower's brewery became part of Whitbread; Aitchison's ('Never Drop Your Aitchies'), a North-Eastern favourite from across the border, fell to Bass Charrington.

products, have established a characteristic visual and verbal idiom, which corporations in no other area have rivalled. Their images and slogans have won a place in the consumers' consciousness which should be the envy of all other advertisers. One means of achieving this has been simple – to decorate the public house – but the very tone of brewery publicity in its many forms reflects the confident swagger with which the drink companies have gone about their business.

The marketing names that have endured, the living legends on the mirrors, evidence the early upsurge of commercial brewing in England, right from the widespread acquiescence to the pernicious hop in the late 16th century. In the 1700s improvements in transport and the eventual introduction of steam power to mechanize breweries intensified competition.

Although all beers were local, a few brewing towns gained a wider reputation, not by advertising but by word of mouth. The reputation attached less to the brewers than to their localities. 'Even in distant times,' says John Bickerdyke, in *The Curiosities of Ale and Beer*, 'particular localities became noted for the excellence of their brewers.' He singles out London and Burton-on-Trent for special attention. Not only did the Midland town brew famous pale ales, it also produced an old ale known as 'Burton.' Yorkshire 'Stingo' was another old ale, the subject of an epic poem in which Bacchus was persuaded to switch from wine to beer. With such mythologies at their disposal, brewers have never been lacking in material for publicity. Newcastle also enjoyed an early reputation for strong, old beers, as did the 'Scotch Ale' from across the border in the brewing city of Edinburgh.

The brewers were not short of commercial ambition even in those days, and the ubiquitous Dr Johnson fancied his chances in the business. When a friend who was a brewer died, Dr Johnson was appointed to be an executor, and he tried to carry on the business. Johnson turned out to be a better producer of epigrams than of beer, and had to negotiate the sale of the business before long, 'bustling about with his ink-horn and pen,' according to Bickerdyke. When asked what he considered to be the value of the property, he replied in the style of the hard-selling publicity man: 'We are not here to sell a parcel of boilers and vats, but the potentiality of growing rich beyond the dream of avarice.' The business was sold to Barclay and Perkins, which became a famous name in brewing before finding its way through yet more capitalistic dealings into today's Courage group.

Another of today's major groupings, Bass Charrington, can claim what may be the world's oldest registered trade-mark. The red triangle used in the Bass label was registered when the Trade Mark Act came into force in 1875. For all that a red triangle might in some lands better communicate danger, it has been taken up as a symbol by at least two drink companies, the other

'ALE' ceased centuries ago to mean an unhopped drink, though it is sometimes used to indicate a mild draught. More often, it is simply another way of saying 'beer.' The word 'ale' has a comfortable, broad-vowelled familiarity that pleases drinker and brewers alike. Fine ales are still brewed at Hartford End, though the prominent mention of porter dates this poster. At Ridley's, that dark beverage barely survived the 1914–18 war.

notable example being the Apollinaris mineral-water concern. The red triangle accompanied by the vigorous Bass script appeared in pubs all over England, and still survives, often as the sign of a fine traditional draught beer. Regrettably, the shining black plaque of the companion brew, Worthington, more often signifies a pressured beer.

The Bass brewery company was started during the reign of George III, when Pitt the Younger was Prime Minister, in 1777. It was founded by William Bass, who also owned a carrying company, but the brewery was so successful that he sold his other interest to the Pickford concern. Today, Pickfords, owned by the State, is England's most famous removal company.

By the time its trade-mark was registered, the marketing flair of the brewing company, then headed by the liberal Member of Parliament Michael Bass, had stimulated intense competition among its rivals. Bass in that period was later described as 'the greatest pale ale brewery in the world.' Companies like Bass built their reputation on the hard water in their home town of Burton-on-Trent, which made a distinguished light-coloured beer. Pale ale from Burton became something of an aristocrat among beers, and the lyrical Bickerdyke called it 'that splendid liquid which, when bottled, vies with champagne in its excellence and delicacy of flavour, and beats it altogether out of the field when we take into consideration its sustaining and restorative powers.'

The fame of Burton was celebrated in rather debatable fashion by the rhyme:

> Ne'er tell me of liquors from Spain or from France,
> They may get in your heels and inspire you to dance,
> But the ale of Old Burton if mellow and right
> Will get in your head and inspire you to fight.

The renown of the Midland beers had already spread to London in the early 1600s, but legislation at the end of the century aimed at improving transport opened the way for Burton to become a unique beer-exporting town. Local firms like Allsopp's were pathfinders in establishing a huge British beer trade via the Baltic to Russia. When Russia imposed high import duties in 1822, the sales-minded Burton brewers intensified their attack on the British capital.

The impact of their pale ales on the London market was such that companies from the Southern brewing town of Romford opened breweries in Burton in order to enjoy the benefits of the local water. The Romford brewery of Ind Coope moved into Burton in 1853, and years later took over the great Allsopp company (today, Ind Coope is a principal component of Allied Breweries). Another Romford brewery which set up in Burton was the long-established concern of Truman, Hanbury and Buxton (today linked with Watneys). Ben Truman had been knighted by George III, and one of the Buxton family was

Ten to one it's
GUINNESS
TIME

LUNCHTIME DRINK: The 'Guinness Time' copyline was introduced in 1931, accompanied by a series of horological puns. ('Ten to One it's Guinness Time'; 'It strikes one it's Guinness Time.'). A huge neon clock was erected by Guinness in Piccadilly, London, in 1932, and similar signs went up in cities all over Britain. The phrase 'Meet me under the Guinness clock' passed into everyday speech. At the Festival of Britain, in 1951, a humorous animated clock was installed in Battersea Park, London, and such devices were later seen at various resorts. The costly novelty clocks lasted until the 1960s, and the neon signs were dismantled in the early 1970s. The animals were introduced in 1935, with the seal and the toucan first on the scene. By 1953, Queen Elizabeth's Coronation year, there was no longer any need to identify the product. The animals spoke for themselves.

a distinguished MP who campaigned against the slave-trade and to limit the use of capital punishment. Many brewers of the period also took up political careers; earlier, Samuel Whitbread, son of the founder of another famous brewery, had been a well-known liberal.

The battle between light Burton ales and those darker beers traditionally made with London's softer water had led to some experimentation on the part of brewers in an effort to woo the market. The result was a legendary brew which was central to English beer-drinking for two centuries, yet which is today almost a forgotten name. The brew was called porter, allegedly because of its popularity with manual workers. Its origins are tangled in folklore, but its purpose was to combine the bitterness of pale ale with the strength of old ale and the rich colour of brown ale. Porter was first made in London in the early 1700s, and later spread to the big industrial cities of Northern England, Scotland and Ireland. Only in the latter country did this 'working man's beer' survive changes in social attitudes and fashions. The great Dublin brewery of Arthur Guinness, founded in 1759, switched entirely to porter production in 1799. Today, the name of Guinness instantly evokes the mysterious black brew which is the principal modern manifestation of porter.

From being an English import to Dublin, porter became an Irish export, and one of the country's main revenue-earners. It took time for porter to penetrate the Western outposts of the British Isles. The English import quickly became a serious worry for Dublin's traditional brown-ale brewers, but the drink was slower to establish itself elsewhere in the predominantly-rural country. Most of Ireland was economically-deprived, communications were bad, and the conservative country areas were strongholds of local spirits. By the time Ireland had its own thriving porter industry, the drink had probably reached its peak in England. Over the decades that followed, English brewers slowly succumbed to new fashions in beer, leaving behind a minority of disenfranchised porter-drinkers, who turned to imported Guinness. Having a home-base in its loyal Irish market, Guinness gradually built up a following in England as a speciality drink. In this, it was helped by the waves of Irish immigrants who had left their own impoverished country to do thirsty work in the growing industrial centres of England.

English brewers allowed Guinness into their tied-houses because it was a distinctive product which did not compete directly with their own principal beers, while at the same time complementing the range of drinks available. Nor was Guinness seen in the same light as other competitors, since it had no tied-houses of its own in England. Guinness's ostensible disadvantages – its 'unfashionable' beer and its unique lack of tied-houses – were turned to neat advantage. The Dublin brewery eventually

PUZZLE PICTURE

ROUND ABOUT six o'clock, beer is best . . . three examples (above and facing page) from Britain's first generic advertising campaign, all produced in the 1930s. The Rockwellian painting was originally used on poster sites, though it was still appearing on beer trays in pubs during the 1940s and 1950s. The custom of indicating a beer's quality by stamping a number of 'X' marks on the barrel dates back to monastic brewing; Mr 'XXX' (facing page) was the character used to personalize the 'Beer is Best' campaign. Although the illustration reflects the superb quality of poster art between the wars, this particular design was never used.

became the biggest in the world, and Guinness opened a plant in England in 1936. That plant, In London, today serves the South of England, while the North is still supplied by Dublin. Guinness produced in these two plants is sold on draught as well as being bottled by local brewery companies all over England, and marketed in their houses under a joint label. Guinness has only one house of its own – amid its hopfields on the Kent-Sussex border at Bodiam – but is available in every English pub. It is not sold as porter, but as 'stout,' a name which was originally applied to beers with an exceptionally full body. Most stouts are sweet; Guinness is bitter.

Instead of fading with age, Guinness's promotional skills have endlessly gained new energy. The more that fashion has continued its swing towards beers lighter and lighter in colour, the more Guinness has capitalized upon the contrary cachet of its dark colour.

The history of Guinness is a marketing classic. Guinness is the most famous advertiser in England, as well as being the best-known brand-name. People don't ask for a 'bitter stout,' they ask for 'Guinness.' The maker's name identifies the product in much the way that a 'Hoover' means a vacuum-cleaner in Britain. Guinness could be described as a generic term if the product had any rivals, but in England it barely has. Its competitors have fallen by the wayside, and the occasional new rival which has emerged has so far always failed. No other beer, no cigarette, no tea or coffee, no grocery product, no household gadget, no car, has a brand-name quite as identifiable as that of Guinness. The company is in the questionable position of being better known as an advertiser than it is as a brewer. People who have never tasted Guinness, or never drink at all, can quote its most famous slogans, describe the graphics of its most memorable ads. People who do not know into what category of beverage Guinness falls are aware nonetheless that it is a long, black alcoholic drink.

Paradoxically, Guinness was hesitant to start advertising, because it built such a reputation without generating its own publicity. The drink was mentioned in the letters of Disraeli, the works of Thackeray and Robert Louis Stevenson, and crops up several times in Charles Dickens. A placard advertising Guinness appeared in the original edition of Pickwick Papers, in a drawing of Sam Weller by the famous illustrator Phiz. The beer's name was mis-spelled, with only one 'n,' but that did not inhibit Guinness when the company finally decided to start advertising: the Phiz illustration appeared in one of the first newspaper ads, in 1929.

After Phiz's unintended contribution, Rex Whistler and H. M. Bateman were commissioned to provide illustrations for Guinness advertisements. Although many artists have illustrated Guinness ads – from the political cartoonist Vicky to Erté, in more modern times – the most prolific was John Gilroy. Among

A-DRINKING WE WILL GO ... HUNTING FOR BEER

Britain's most famous huntsman was John Peel, born in Cumbria in 1776. His names lives on in the folk-song, 'D'ye ken (know) John Peel?' The ales named after him (2) were produced by Cumbria's Workington Brewery until the company was taken over by Matthew Brown, of Blackburn, Lancashire, in 1975. The strongest hunting theme among beer brands is pursued by Eldridge, Pope (4), whose symbol has a remarkable counterpart in that of Tetley's (5). Both breweries were sold the same off-the-peg design by a famous printing company in 1922. The brewers soon discovered this, but carried on regardless, since their marketing areas are at opposite ends of the country. Eldridge, Pope had already registered the trade-name 'Huntsman Ales' for their Dorset brews.

JOHN PEEL ALES

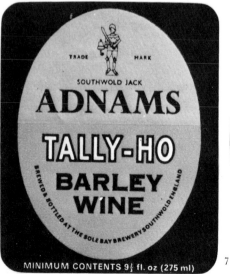

the copywriters used by Guinness was Dorothy L. Sayers, creator of the English detective Lord Peter Wimsey.

Even in 1929, Guinness found a 'hot' ad agency. Its best known slogan, *Guinness is Good for You*, turns out to be the product of research. So many respondents made the assertion that both the client and agency wondered whether it wasn't too obvious. The ease with which it tripped off the tongue, backed by its essential accuracy, made it into one of advertising's greatest copylines. The slogan provided the basis for an exclamatory style of advertising that has rarely flagged. *My Goodness, My Guinness* introduced a series of adventures involving a zoo-keeper, a glass of stout, and a menagerie of animals, which became corporate characters over the years. The graphic colour and strength of the animals was such that they were eventually used with no copy whatever – not even the Guinness logo – in a 1953 Coronation-year poster. Just as the animals outgrew their original context, so the whole of Guinness advertising became highly allusive. When the public were baffled by a poster, they wrote to Guinness for an explanation, and occasionally involved the company in extremely esoteric dialogues.

The theme of Guinness as a health drink extended to another series of posters, remembered years later in the advertising-industry magazine *Campaign*: 'That man carrying the girder still walks confidently in the minds of millions who grew up between the wars. Who could forget a claim as sound and succinct as *Guinness Gives You Strength?' Campaign* made the comment in a tribute, written almost in the style of an obituary, when the advertising account left the Benson agency after a record 40 years. Guinness had helped Benson's to become one of the first really big British agencies, and the firm never wholly recovered from the loss of the account. Around the same time, Benson's lost one of the big banks, and the Bovril meat extract account, which had also provided some historic graphics in its heyday. Soon afterwards, Benson's was merged into the American agency founded by Britain's most famous adman, David Ogilvy. Guinness moved to the world's biggest agency, J. Walter Thompson, whose London office had enjoyed particular success. JWT's early work for the new client suggested that the agency might well rise to the challenge of Guinness.

The impact of World War I, the temperance movement and the economic crises of the 1920s and 1930s evoked a spectre unusual in England: falling beer sales. The reply of the brewers made advertising history. They launched a well-remembered joint advertising campaign over the slogan, *Beer is Best*. 'When you buy beer,' the errant public was reminded, 'you benefit yourself, the British farmer and the British Exchequer.' This public-spirited tone continued after 1939, when the brewers donated their campaign space to the Ministry of Information for the war effort, with a series of ads answering the questions, 'What

Tetley's huntsman used to hang outside their pubs in Yorkshire, but has been relegated to a lesser role since they became part of Allied Breweries in the 1960s. The hunting cry of Tally Ho! persists elsewhere in Dorset (a county famous for the sport), on the label of Palmer's Strong Ale (6). The East Anglians see Tally-Ho as a barley wine, and disagree on punctuation (7). Adnams' interest in hunting dates back at least to 1898 (1), and McMullens' (3) to the 1930s. The motif is irresistible to brewers, eager as they are to evoke rural images (beer, being made of barley and hops, is a country drink . . .); hunts meet at pubs; and John Barleycorn, personification of beer, sometimes wears hunting pink.

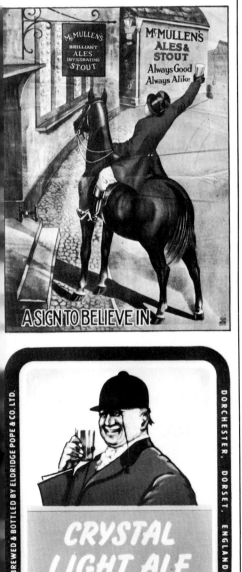

HARTLEYS PALE ALE
BREWED AND BOTTLED IN GREAT BRITAIN
MIN. Contents 19¼ Fluid ozs.

BATEMAN'S B·B·B BEER
GEO. BATEMAN & SON LTD
SALEM BRIDGE BREWERY
WAINFLEET
THIS BOTTLE IS USED AS A MEANS OF CONVEYING BEER AND IS NOT GUARANTEED TO BE IMPERIAL MEASURE

RUTLAND BARLEY WINE
BREWED & BOTTLED IN GT BRITAIN BY G RUDDLE & CO LTD THE BREWERY, LANGHAM, OAKHAM, RUTLAND
MINIMUM CONTENTS 8·8 fl.oz/250 ml

OLDHAM BREWERY FAMOUS PALE OB ALE
REGISTERED TRADE MARK
MINIMUM CONTENTS 9⅔ FL. OZ.
OLDHAM

Badger XXXX OLD ENGLISH ALE
MINIMUM CONTENTS 9⅘ fl. oz. 27.44 cl.
ESTABLISHED 1777
BREWED & BOTTLED BY HALL & WOODHOUSE LTD
BLANDFORD · ENGLAND

Rayment's Coronation Ale
The Queen God Bless Her
BREWED AND BOTTLED AT THE BREWERY FURNEUX PELHAM HERTS

WADWORTH'S CORONATION OF ELIZABETH II QUEEN'S ALE
BREWED & BOTTLED AT NORTHGATE BREWERY DEVIZES

BATEMAN'S BOTTLED BY THE BREWERS NUT BROWN WAINFLEET
THIS BOTTLE IS USED AS A MEANS OF CONVEYING BEER AND IS NOT GUARANTEED TO BE

WADWORTH & CO LTD
NORTH GATE TRADE MARK DEVIZES
Wadworth & Co Ltd
BROWN ALE
NORTHGATE BREWERY. DEVIZES
THIS LABEL IS ISSUED ONLY BY
WADWORTH & CO LTD NORTHGATE BREWERY, DEVIZES

Abbot Ale
GREENE KING
Brewed at Bury St. Edmunds, England.

GRAY & SONS BREWERS LIMITED BROWN ALE
SPRINGFIELD ROAD BREWERY
CHELMSFORD

Old Nick YOUNG'S BARLEY WINE
Young & Co's Brewery Ltd London UK Minimum Contents 6 Fl Oz 170 ml

SPECIAL LUNCHEON ALE
BREWED AND BOTTLED BY THE HOME BREWERY CO. LTD., DAYBROOK, NOTTS., ENGLAND
MINIMUM CONTENTS 19½ fl oz/550 ml

Anchor Export Beer
Brewed and Bottled for Export by THE HULL BREWERY CO. LTD., ENGLAND

Devenish Crabbers' NIP
MIN. CONTENTS 6⅓ FLUID OZS.

GUINNESS'S EXTRA STOUT
BOTTLED AND GUARANTEED BY
G. BATEMAN & SON LTD BREWERS Wine & Spirit Merchants WAINFLEET
DUBLIN
THIS BOTTLE IS USED AS A MEANS OF CONVEYING BEER AND IS NOT GUARANTEED TO BE

THE PECULIARITIES of beer labels, past and present, are infinite (preceding pages and above). Take the strange case of Old Peculier. This unusual strong beer is named after the peculier (sic) powers of the local ecclesiastical court. The top label makes a half-hidden gesture to the peculier spelling in the tiny seal, but gives prominence to a more conventional rendition. This changed when the beer began to gain a reputation beyond its parochial confines in the early 1970s. The brewers decided at that point to promote its antiquity with more vigour, by restoring the archaic spelling to pride of place. Thus the older label is the more modern in spelling, and the more modern label the older, so to speak. No such devious paths are trodden by the brewers of Bateman's Good, Honest Ales (facing page). Their staff can pose for the Lincolnshire brewery's centenary photograph with a clear conscience.

do I do about fire bombs . . . if my home is hit . . . if it is reported that the Germans have landed?' In the austerity period after the war, the English faced the new experience of a beer shortage, and the renewal of supplies had to be trumpeted with a new *Beer is Best* campaign.

Beer is Best has been claimed as the first-ever generic campaign for a whole industry, and such exercises became fashionable in post-war England. The most successful, *Drinka Pinta*, should have been for beer, but was for milk. In the years since, advertising has all but drowned in its own heady sophistication. One of the most popularly quoted campaigns, *I'm only here for the beer*, deliberately made no claim for the product it was supposed to be selling. People bandied about the slogan, but could barely remember to which beer it referred – *Double Diamond*.

Brewers have traditionally been less reticent, and many of them retain their homespun confidence. 'The Beer with the Glow' is brewed by Holden's of Dudley; 'The beer with the strength of a lion' by Morrell's of Oxford, though presumably the same could be said for Lion Ales, made by Blackburn's Matthew Brown. In the North-East, Cameron's ('Strongarm') claim 'The mightiest of beers'; Vaux ('Brewed in the North for people who know good beer') have a brand called Samson; Sam Smith's have used the name Old Samson; and fellow Yorkshiremen Webster's have a character called Young Sam. Hardy's and Hanson's of Nottingham ('Stop with the hop') have a beer called Old Kim; Eldridge, Pope, in Dorset, have Old Master (and a beer named Thomas Hardy); Oldham Brewery has Old Tom; Marston, Evershed, of Burton has Owd Roger; McMullen's of Hertford ('Good beer – great pubs') has Olde Time; Young's in London, devilishly prefer Old Nick. Such notions are countered by the pious brewers of Eastern England, with Abbot Ale and St Edmund's Ale (Greene, King); Bishop Ale (Ridley's); Bishop's Finger (Shepherd Neame); and Cardinal Ale (Tollemache and Cobbold); none of which beats Oh Be Joyful!, brewed by Dutton's, part of the Whitbread group, in Blackburn. Both Tetley's of Leeds and Eldridge, Pope uses a huntsman logo; while the Workington Brewery calls its beers after John Peel; Palmers, in Dorset, and Adnams, in Suffolk, both have beers called Tally Ho! The Home Brewery Company of Nottingham has beers called Robin Hood and Little John; John Willie Lees of Manchester has Archer Stout; Greenall, Whitley of Warrington has Bullseye brown ale. St Austell brewery has Smuggler's Ale; Devenish, in Dorset, has Crabber's Nip.

Simple country virtues have been a good measure of England's beers since the days when Richard II ordered brewers to identify themselves by erecting 'ale-stakes.' The king's peripatetic 'ale-conners' allegedly submitted each new brew to the 'trousers test.' They poured a little beer on to a bench, and sat in it until it dried. If it was sufficiently strong, the conner's leather breeches would stick slightly to the bench as he got up. If the ale was not sticky enough, the brewer might be ordered to drink the whole consignment, or have it poured over him. Which of today's claims for beer could match that simple product-demonstration? Has Madison Avenue ever produced a 'show'n'tell' tv commercial quite that effective?

And which advertising man has made such a convincing argument for beer as the saddler of Nottingham? He was condemned to the gallows for the offence which he claimed not to have committed. On the way from Newgate Jail to the executioner at Tyburn, he was offered the customary last glass of beer, at the *White Hart*, in Drury Lane. Unable to stomach the thought of beer at a time like that, he waved-on the tumbrel-driver, and arrived for hanging two or three minutes early. His corpse was still twitching at the end of the rope when a pardon arrived. Apocryphal, maybe, but the message is clear: never refuse a beer – it may save your life.

BY HENRY POOLE. R.A.

ED. UP

Mahogany and Marble

Architecture and interiors

LAVISH CARVING, alabaster, mosaic, copper panelling, bronze tableaux and ironwork crowd round the incomparable Black Friar, decorating exterior and interior, alcoves and ingle-nook. The pub, in its Arts and Crafts style, is a teasing triumph, alive with unexpected strokes of wit. The theme is the good life allegedly enjoyed by the friars. The endless carvings and bas-reliefs are captioned with mottoes: 'A good thing is soon snatched up' (left), 'Don't advertise – tell a gossip,' 'Wisdom is rare,' 'Haste is slow' . . .

BEFORE THE QUEEN made him her official poet in 1972, Sir John Betjeman had an unofficial public role as the protector of all that was good in England. On one occasion, he campaigned to save a London pub called the *Black Friar*, which was threatened with demolition to make way for a road scheme. The pub was not well-known, and its Victorian and Edwardian architecture was of a style frequently derided at the time. Nor was Sir John the first man to have cared about a beautiful pub, but his success was perhaps a sign that the English at large were prepared to take a greater interest in the architecture of their drinking houses.

The *Black Friar* is a symbol of all that is individualistic and grand in the English pub. With all around it rent asunder, it stands in solitary splendour: 'the finest example of turn-of-the-century *Art Nouveau* design in London,' according to the book *City of London Pubs*; 'the best pub in the Arts and Crafts fashion in London,' as Sir Nikolaus Pevsner, Britain's best-known architectural historian, would have it. The pub's pink, green and white veined marble, its alabaster figures, its coal fire and inglenooks and – above all – its lavish copper and bronze, its friezes depicting bacchanalia among the friars who gave the place its name; all of this is unique, even among other houses of the period. The *Black Friar* was constructed in 1875, and extensively rebuilt in 1905 by H. Fuller Clark. Further additions were made in the years from 1919 to 1924 by Clark, with sculptures by H. Poole and A. T. Bradford. Their names hardly ring loud in the history of architecture, but together they elevated the English pub even at its height to a new pinnacle of style and extravagance.

On the same site, there was a Dominican monastery in the 13th century, and the whole area has long been known as Blackfriars. The fading railway station that bears the same name stands nearby, remembering how it once dispatched passengers to a random list of European cities and English towns: Genoa,

THE INSCRIPTIONS which announce the Black Friar personify its style: The fine detail is the quality that makes the pub so remarkable. At first glance, the Black Friar withholds its full range of expression, as if intimidated by its uncomfortable surroundings. The Salisbury, on the other hand (facing page) proclaims itself in lights fit for theatre-land . . . a last flourish of the swanky 1890s in the West End of London.

Baden-Baden, Brindisi and Ashford; Florence, Leipzig, and Westgate-on-Sea; Darmstadt, Berlin, St. Petersburg and Crystal Palace. Once they had started pulling the neighbourhood apart, Blackfriars Station got its share of troubles, too. But the stone-carved destination lists that have befuddled many a home-going drinker from the *Black Friar* will be restored to their place when the station is rebuilt. Behind the station is the *Mermaid* theatre of Sir Bernard Miles; across the Thames, via Blackfriars Bridge, is Southwark ('more intimately London than any other borough,' in the words of Pevsner), the home of the Shakespearean *George*.

More than one pub-crawl could be planned from the *Black Friar*, though it had best be at lunchtime or early evening. Many houses in the City area close early at night. No square mile in England has a greater number of historic pubs. Some are outstanding, most of them at the very least are interesting, but it is their numbers and their concentration that makes the City such a rewarding area for the aesthetic drinker. A high proportion of the good City pubs feature in the *Good Beer Guide*: Near St. Paul's is the *Watling*, built in 1662 and restored this century, where the Society for the Preservation of Beers from the Wood was founded. Near Leadenhall Market, and dating back originally to the 13th century, is the *Hoop and Grapes*. At Smithfield, the *Bishop's Finger* has Shepherd, Neame beer and a good restaurant. Fleet Street has the 17th-century *Cheshire Cheese*, the *Punch*, and the *Old Bell*.

Because the capital grew from the City and the Pool of London, its oldest pubs are there, several of them dating back to the reconstruction that followed the Great Fire of 1666. In today's centre, the West End, an 'old' pub is more likely to be Victorian. Two in particular illustrate – along with the *Black Friar* – the architectural range of the pub in its golden age. The most lavish is the *Salisbury*, in St. Martin's Lane, described by Pevsner as 'a well-preserved, ornate Late Victorian pub, with plenty of cut and frosted glass, a Lincrusta ceiling, curved leather-

PRIVACY is still afforded by snob-screens (right), at the Bunch of Grapes, in Brompton Road, London. The screens, at head-height on the bar, can be opened when the customer wishes to be served, then closed to shield him from the view of others or shut out his conversation. There is argument about the origins of the device, but it was probably provided for the drinker who wished to be discreet during the late 19th century, when the respectability of pubs was being called into question. Such intimate touches contrast with the towering scale of a pub built only a decade or two later. The Vines (facing page), in Liverpool, is a palatial example of Edwardian baroque.

covered seats arranged in a row so as to form shallow niches, and several small *Art Nouveau* bronze figures of alluring maidens in conjunction with flower stalks and flowers, out of which grow electric bulbs. There could hardly be a more camp environment for the predominantly-male clientele of this pub, in the heart of theatre-land; it is a spectacular place, which no enthusiast for either Victoriana or pubs should miss. By comparison, the *Red Lion*, between Jermyn Street and St. James' Square, is neat and tiny. This pub, packed from wall to wall with cut-glass mirrors and mahogany, has been described as 'a perfect example of the small Victorian gin-palace at its best.'

The glories of London are so many that 'redevelopment' was allowed to proceed with barely a care in the 1950s and 1960s. For a city that hit its peak of energy and enterprise during the late Victorian era, the capital has shamefully few pubs that recall their own most confident period. Dickens wrote that developers were 'depositing splendid mansions, stone balustrades, rosewood fittings, immense lamps, and illustrated clocks, at the corner of every street.' Some years ago, regulars at Dickens' old local, in Lamb's Conduit Street, Bloomsbury, had a rather different experience. Their pub, the *Lamb*, was 'renovated.' The public bar was torn down, and with it went the 'snob screens' – revolving glass partitions intended to shield from working-class customers and staff alike the privileged conversation of the saloon-bar drinkers. The customers protested with all the invective that might be expected from literary Bloomsbury, and the pub's owners put the screens back. The brewery in question, Young's, is well known for its sensitivity to tradition.

Some of the Late Victorian pubs outside the heart of London have better survived the hammer of destruction, despite the scorn of Ruskin, who complained that there was 'scarcely a public house near Crystal Palace but sells its gin-and-bitters under pseudo-Venetian capitals.' The one-time suburbs that

now ring Central London – Maida Vale is a good example – have many delightful locals dating back to Victorian times. These areas also have some architectural eccentricities among their pubs, because a 'picturesque' style was sometimes thought appropriate for residential neighbourhoods. The original *Swiss Cottage* was built for that reason.

Many of the most extravagant Victorian and Edwardian pubs are nowhere near the capital. 'Everyone remarks the increase in gin-shops,' wrote Edward Gibbon Wakefield, in 1833, 'in all those parts of Leeds or Manchester . . . where the poorest people live. There you find, in almost every dirty street, not one but several fine houses, handsomely stuccoed, curiously painted, ornamented with plate-glass and polished brass . . . inside, great barrels of spirits gaily painted and disposed for show, carved mahogany and more polished brass.'

Leeds, with a stern pride reflecting the characters of the Yorkshire woolmasters, still has a few Victorian and Edwardian pubs. The best-loved and most unusual is *Whitelocks*', a low-ceilinged tavern which was converted into a luncheon bar just after the turn of the century. The boom in 'dining rooms' in the second half of the 1800s is not especially apparent in today's London pubs, but this Yorkshire version is a stylish venue for lunchtime drinking. It has a tiled counter, *Art Nouveau* stained glass, and a variety of embellishments.

Of all the great industrial cities in the North and Midlands, Manchester was perhaps the richest in Victorian architecture, but it has also been one of the most enthusiastic with the bulldozer. In his book *Victorian Pubs*, Mark Girouard commends the Gothic *Crown and Kettle*, on Oldham Road, but there are dozens of smaller pubs in the Manchester area which have beautiful stained-glass, cut-glass and tiling.

Some big provincial cities produced pubs as grand as, or

DEEP, rich colours, filtered light, and partition into smaller areas, can give even the largest pub a quality of warmth, cosiness, almost intimacy. The tactile qualities of moulded plasterwork, carved wood, burnished windows, embossed wallpapers like Lincrusta, and delicate metalwork, add a sense of comfortable well-being. The glitter of the early-Victorian gin-palace gradually mellowed into the lavish comfort of the Edwardian pubs. Caryatids at the Sawyers' Arms in Manchester (far left, top), the Vines, in Liverpool (top, right) and the same city's Philharmonic (above). Glasswork at the Central, Liverpool (far left, bottom); gaslight fitting at the Vines.

THE GABLES of the Philharmonic (top and facing page) crown an exterior which perhaps merits the description 'Pont Street Dutch,' a style invented by cartoonist and designer Osbert Lancaster. He was talking about the street in Chelsea, but there are some fine examples of the style in Liverpool. Brian Spiller describes 'very free variants of the post-Gothic fashion, applied to convey liveliness without loss of respectability.' The gables, and a mighty turret, recur in the Vines.

grander than, London. One possible reason for this is the fact that brewers were so well able to organize the tied-house system in provincial cities; with less opposition, they could more easily develop their outlets, the pubs. In Liverpool particularly – perhaps because it was a port city, with a very transient population – licensees were predominantly men employed by brewers as managers, rather than being tenants. The brewers there consequently had an especially strong control over their houses, and used them effectively as lavish and memorable advertisements.

In Birmingham, Girouard describes the *Barton Arms*, at Aston, as 'gorgeous . . . more like a small town-hall than a pub. The ceilings are lined with tiles by Minton, Hollins and Company, of Stoke-on-Trent. The smoking rooms and lobby are rich in stained glass, elaborate chimney-pieces, and bronze light brackets, and the bars in embossed glass.'

Liverpool is, though, the home city of the lavish public house. The most famous Liverpool pub is the *Philharmonic*, with the *Vines* and the *Central* enjoying widespread admiration. There are also a good many lesser houses worthy of note, especially for their *Art Nouveau* features. The pub that rose between 1898 and 1900 opposite Liverpool's Philharmonic Hall has an exterior which Girouard describes as, 'Queen Anne, turning into free classic.' Another expert, Brian Spiller, talks about the interior in *Victorian Public Houses:* 'Still remarkably Ninetyish in atmosphere, with a flavour of *Art Nouveau:* plaster caryatids, a curving bar counter faced with crimson and gold mosaic, repoussé copper panels, and heavily moulded plasterwork. Light filters through screens and windows of stained glass, patterned with coats-of-arms, celebrating contemporary heroes.'

The *Vines*, in legend-laden Lime Street, was built in 1907. Its exterior is described by Girouard as, 'free classic, turning into Edwardian baroque.' Spiller talks about 'shirt-front architecture . . . billowing gables, and giant, upthrusting turret.' Of the interior, he says: 'A combination of engraved glass and carved mahogany, ornate plasterwork and stained glass, continues a tradition of late Victorian craftsmanship into its Edwardian afterglow.'

The third of Liverpool's three great pubs is opposite Central Station, from which it takes its name. Once more, Spiller is lyrical: 'The walls of the front bar have a dado of green tiles, decorated with an enigmatic flowing pattern in the *Art Nouveau* manner. Above it, leading the eye upwards to an ornate, many-coloured dome, arcaded panels of engraved glass isolate the customers from the din and turmoil of the street, enveloping them in filtered light.'

'The exteriors of Victorian public houses,' says Spiller, 'were designed to bring the customers in, and the interiors to encourage them to remain.' The result may not have been

HANDSOME TABLE,

*MASSIVE
BRONZED STAND.*

26-in. Circular Mahogany
or Marble Tops, 22,6 each.

Similar, with 24-inch Tops,
21/- each.

22-inch Tops, 18/- each.

BRITISH-MADE, and built to last . . . A piece of furniture which would be identified instantly as a 'pub table' by any regular drinker. The 'Britannia table' dates back beyond the turn of the century, and is still widely used. The cast-iron tables are substantial, decorative, and a characteristic part of the pub scene. Britain's heroes have proved to be less durable. Field Marshall Lord Roberts (facing page) is less than a household name today. He was a contemporary hero at the time of the Philharmonic's construction, and survives in the pub's stained-glass windows.

regarded as 'good taste' in its time, but has been described as 'a rich substitute – popular architecture.' The imperatives that guided brewers in the design of their pubs were also felt by the creators of restaurants and theatres in the same period, and these places of leisure together gave rise to their own genre of architecture, which usually employed a bizarre combination of styles. They combine and contrast still, in the main streets of almost every English town, with a tiled hall here and a marble-and-mahogany monument there, all pillars and posts, too often being slowly degraded into a plastic palace. Add a touch of intoxication to a walk down the English high-street, and a pub-crawl is a trip indeed.

One reaction to the vulgarity of the typical Victorian house was a movement for 'improved' pubs, which tried to reincarnate the nobler mood of the best and most restful country inn. The archetypal example of this 'Queen Anne' style is set in one of those curious mock-rural suburbs which were a product of the same thinking. The *Tabard* – even its name harks back to the Chaucerian inn – is at Bedford Park, between Hammersmith and Chiswick, in West London. Although Norman Shaw's interior has not survived intact, tiles by De Morgan and Walter Crane are still much in evidence. The 'Queen Anne' style also survives at the other end of town, in the *Connaught* and *Galleons*, at Albert Docks. Hand-in-hand with 'Queen Anne' went 'Old English,' which can be seen at the nearby *Ship*, in Victoria Docks.

Of the architects who followed this style in later years, Girouard says: 'Their exteriors favoured roughcast and low eaves; their interiors looked clean and bright, with plenty of scrubbed oak and exposed brickwork, oak settles in the ingle-nook, and Windsor chairs scattered across tiled floors.' This school, however, had less worthy imitators who 'gloried in half-timbered gables, leaded lights, bottle-glass lanterns, wooden barrels, carved black oak, and artificially-smoked ceilings between artificially-warped beams.' He quotes the present *Cock* in Fleet Street, several Younger's houses, and a great many suburban pubs built throughout England during the 1920s and 1930s.

Brewers' Tudor is a term well understood among architects, so it could be argued that pub-designers created a style which passed into wider use. Not only have some pubs emerged almost as textbook examples – the *Grove*, at Dulwich, London, is a case in point – but other buildings have adopted the mode, too. There is a bank in the Manchester suburb of Didsbury which feigns the manner with such success that it is often mistaken for a pub. 'Brewers' Tudor' was also the last definable style to be applied to pubs on a nationwide basis. Many towns have distinctive houses which evidence the work of a single architect at the local brewery during one period or

GENUINE TIMBERING (top), in Tewkesbury, Gloucestershire. Although the style is commonly described as being Tudor, 'Gloster's Oldest Inn' was built in 1308, before that family came to the throne. ('Gloster' is a centuries-old abbreviation which happens to echo the pronunciation of the county's name.) A typical example of the 'Brewers' Tudor' pubs built in the 1930s is the Mitre (above), at Norwich. In this case, the 1934 reproduction façade was imposed in the rebuilding of a much older house.

another, but there is no sign that the modern pub is making a cohesive impact on English architecture.

The earliest pubs were merely homes that sold beer, and for several centuries, the alcoholic architecture of England was the country's domestic building style. The aspirants to the title of England's first drinking house are several: Origins as early as the year 560 have been claimed for *Ye Olde Ferry Boat Inn*, at Holywell, in Cambridgeshire. There is some evidence that it pre-dates the local church, built in 980, but the earliest documents are dated 1100. The *Fighting Cocks*, at St. Albans, Hertfordshire, is on an eighth-century site, though its present structure is an 11th-century building. Church records at Bardsey, near Leeds, Yorkshire, suggest that a 'Priest's Inn' existed in the year 905, and it may have been the original from which the present *Bingley Arms* was developed in 1738. The *Godbegot*, in Winchester, Hampshire, dates back to 1002. The *Trip to Jerusalem*, in Nottingham, has foundations believed to date back to 1070. The *Angel and Royal*, at Grantham, Lincolnshire, has cellar masonry dated 1213, and the building itself was erected around 1450. The *George*, at Norton St. Philip, Somerset, was built in the early 15th century.

The country pub's pastiche of architectural styles reflects

THE ALCOHOLIC ARCHITECTURE OF ENGLAND

Weather-boarding, or clapper-boarding, in Kent, at the General Wolfe, Westerham (his birthplace). The style is common in West Kent and throughout Sussex.

Tile-hanging, especially on the upper storeys of houses, is also common to Kent and Sussex, and especially the town of Lewes. The Henry VIII is at Hever, Kent.

Pantiled roofs are common in Norfolk. The Black Lion is in that county, at Walsingham. The tiles are also found in other parts of England, especially the South.

Thatching is found all over England. While the reeds used come from Norfolk, less exposed counties have more thatching. The Wise Man is near Dorchester.

Timbering manifests itself in the styles of several periods and regions. Very decorative timbering is common in Cheshire and Shropshire. The Feathers is at Ludlow.

Stone buildings, sturdy and symmetrical, are characteristic of Northern Yorkshire, Durham, Northumberland and Cumbria. The Clickham is near Penrith, Cumbria.

the periods through which it has passed since the days of the Saxon ale-house. Between the trim thatch and the spruce white-wash there also resides a multiplicity of local building techniques: pubs may be weather-boarded or tile-hung in Kent and Sussex; pargeted (decorated on the outside with raised plasterwork) in Suffolk; pebbled in Norfolk; perhaps even Dutch-gabled in Lincolnshire; basking in mellow Cotswold limestone, or sturdy in the grit sandstones of Yorkshire and County Durham.

Thatched pubs soften many an English landscape, though they are scarce in the more exposed North. The East has a fair scatter – including the Lincolnshire territories of two excellent brewers, Bateman's and Sam Smith's – bearing witness to the proximity of England's main source of thatching reeds, amid the waterways and lakes of Norfolk. Perhaps the heartlands of thatched England are gentle Southern counties like Hampshire, Wiltshire and, especially, Dorset.

For a small county, Dorset has a lot to offer along with its thatch: the settings for the stories of Thomas Hardy; prehistoric sites, and the phallic Cerne Abbas Giant; some spectacular geological oddities; and, last but hardly least, no less than four independent local breweries. A leading claimant to the distinc-

tion of being England's smallest pub is a thatched house in Dorset – the *Smith's Arms*, serving the county's Devenish beer, at Godmanstone, near Dorchester. The Dorset brewery of Hall and Woodhouse offers a thatched pub called the *Crown*, at Sturminster Newton, which is said to have been Hardy's model for the *Pure Drop Inn*, in *Tess of the D'Urbervilles*.

Hardy's towns and villages are identified in a map produced by another of Dorset's brewers, Eldridge, Pope. To help evoke the images of the author's part-real, part-imaginary Wessex, the brewery also produces a potent *Thomas Hardy's Ale*. This drink was once listed by the *Guinness Book of Records* as the world's strongest beer – a rare tribute from one brewer to another. Correspondence between Thomas Hardy and the company's Mr Pope survives, but sentiment has been less kind to the original Mr Eldridge. The house of which he was once licensee, the *Antelope Hotel*, in Dorchester, is now served by another brewery.

The *Antelope* is more noteworthy architecturally, as a good, if late, manifestation of the coaching inn. It was built in about 1815 (Pevsner describes its façade as 'a very happy composition'), at a time when surfaced roads were bringing a boom to the coaching trade. Within a couple of decades, the boom was in railway-building, Brunel was forging West, and coaching inns were experiencing hard times. Like many such inns which survived those difficulties, the *Antelope* remains true to its origins; it regards its prime role today as that of a medium-sized hotel, though it is also used as a pub. Dorchester has another good example of the coaching inn, the older *King's Arms*, complete

THE WHITEWASHED wall, the signpost to catch the passing eye . . . low lies that house where nut-brown draughts inspire. Neither the vintage of humour nor the architectural style of the village pub has changed much since Goldsmith's day. Rural locals are still most often in the building style of the district's homes, embellished by repair or extension over the years. Left: the New Inn, at Coleford, Devon.

SELECTIONS FROM GOLDSMITH'S "DESERTED VILLAGE"
THE VILLAGE ALE-HOUSE.

NEAR YONDER THORN THAT LIFTS ITS HEAD ON HIGH,
WHERE ONCE THE SIGN-POST CAUGHT THE PASSING EYE,
LOW LIES THAT HOUSE WHERE NUT-BROWN DRAUGHTS INSPIRED,
WHERE GRAY-BEARD MIRTH AND SMILING TOIL RETIRED,
WHERE VILLAGE STATESMEN TALKED WITH LOOKS PROFOUND,
AND NEWS MUCH OLDER THAN THEIR ALE WENT ROUND.
IMAGINATION FONDLY STOOPS TO TRACE,
THE PARLOUR-SPLENDOURS OF THAT FESTIVE PLACE;
THE WHITE-WASHED WALL, THE NICELY SANDED FLOOR,
THE VARNISHED CLOCK THAT CLICKED BEHIND THE DOOR;

THE CHEST CONTRIVED A DOUBLE DEBT TO PAY,
A BED BY NIGHT, A CHEST OF DRAWERS BY DAY;
THE PICTURES PLACED FOR ORNAMENT AND USE,
THE TWELVE GOOD RULES, THE ROYAL GAME OF GOOSE;
THE HEARTH, EXCEPT WHEN WINTER CHILLED THE DAY,
WITH ASPEN BOUGHS AND FLOWERS AND FENNEL GAY;
WHILE BROKEN TEA-CUPS WISELY KEPT FOR SHOW,
RANGED O'ER THE CHIMNEY GLISTENED IN A ROW.

with arched carriage entrance, and horseman's mounting-blocks. The *King's Arms* also has associations with Hardy; he did a great deal of writing there, and used the place when he wished to entertain.

The inns of Dorchester typify those which are an identifiable feature of towns on old coaching routes the length and breadth of England. At the opposite end of the country, Ripon is another attractive and historic little town which offers several examples of the style, with the characteristic coaching arches. One of Ripon's most pleasant coaching inns, the *Black Bull*, omits the arch, but compensates by offering the visitor the rare and distinctive *Old Peculier*. The name of this North Yorkshire brew might be thought quite appropriate to a town which retains its hornblower. Every evening at 9.0, he sounds what was once the curfew, but the pubs happily ignore this injunction.

UNDERNEATH THE ARCHES ... TRAVEL IN THE EARLY 1800s

The Coaching Inn: To the vehicles which thundered across England, the inn was a place where passengers could eat, sleep, embark. Many of the towns which were important points on the network are now by-passed by motorway and rail, but they still reveal their former role. The arch, through which the vehicle drove to park, identifies the Saracen's Head, in Ripon, Yorkshire, as a coaching inn. Nor has the George and Pilgrims, in Glastonbury, Somerset, changed much externally since its period as the George Hotel. The Coach and Horses remains a popular pub name. The one on the far right is in Sherborne, Dorset.

The colour of Old England is perhaps best recalled by those pubs timbered in the black-and-white Tudor fashion. Timbered inns in a variety of local styles still stand all over England, from the 15th-century *Star*, in Alfriston, Sussex, to the *Wellington*, in the centre of Manchester. The latter, believed to have been built in the 14th century, has been splendidly preserved amid the ravages of Manchester's 'redevelopment.' The part of the country richest in timbering is the West Midlands: places like Tewkesbury, in Gloucestershire; Ledbury, in Herefordshire (with the delightfully-named *Trumpet Inn*, at Pixley); and especially Shrewsbury, county town of Shropshire. (The name 'Shropshire' has an English country softness, much more welcoming than the Anglo-Norman 'Salop,' which the administrators prefer.)

Shrewsbury is one of England's two superb Tudor towns (as well as being the birthplace of Darwin). It has two outstanding timbered inns, both of which win the rare praise of Pevsner: the *Golden Cross*, 'probably pre-Reformation,' and the *King's Head* (15th or early 16th century). The Earl of Shrewsbury once lived in a building which is now a pub, but that is in the 'rival' Tudor town of Chester, 30 or 40 miles further North.

Chester spans three periods. It is a walled Roman city; it has some exquisite medieval buildings, notably its galleried shops known as 'The Rows'; but it also has a considerable amount of Victorian reproduction timbering, freer in style and grander in scale than the original. The Earl's town-house, however, is a lovely 17th-century building now better known as the *Bear and Billet*. Another inn, the *Old King's Head*, was once the home of the Chester Herald (an office of royal ceremonial) and the city's Mayor. The *Old King's Head* was built in 1598 and restored in 1750; the *Nag's Head* was built in 1597 and restored in 1914; the *Pied Bull*, with 16th or early 17th work in the interior, was rebuilt in the 18th century; the *Royal Oak* was built in 1601 and rebuilt in 1920; and the *Yacht Inn*, built in the 17th century, displays the rare distinction of graffiti by Swift.

The idiosyncrasies of English pub architecture knew no bounds. In Brighton, a fine town for idiosyncrasy, the *Hanbury Arms* and *Bombay Bar* reside beneath a pagoda roof in a building which was created as a mausoleum for the Sassoons, a great family of Imperial England. The same town has a *Henekey's* pub described by Pevsner as 'wonderfully phoney . . . even with a portcullis.' The *Puzzle Hall*, at Sowerby Bridge, near Halifax, West Yorkshire, is a towered pub that once brewed its own beer. The *Crooked House*, near Dudley, in the West Midlands, lives up to its name; every surface or fixed object in the pub is crooked. Oddest of all is the *Pack of Cards*, at Combe Martin, Devon, built by a local squire after a spectacular gambling success. Its four floors represent the four suits; it has 13 doors, and 52 windows.

Of such eccentricity are Englishmen made, and nowhere do they express it better than in their pubs.

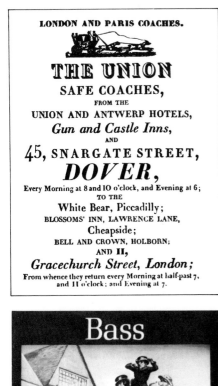

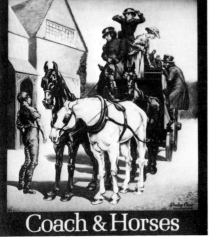

Playing the Game

Sports and contests

O F THE 40-ODD sports and games played inside and outside the pub, is any odder than cricket? Unbelievably, some are. But none is as English as the national summer sport. Every land which ever flew the Union Jack has cricket among its souvenirs of Imperial rule, and expatriates to dream of summer days, tankard of beer in hand, waiting for rain to stop play. The image would be incomplete without the pint of beer, which is as much a part of the reverie as bat, ball, and stumps.

Most village cricket grounds are within batting distance of the 'local,' and countless pubs are named after the sport. Londoners who retreat to the Surrey countryside can visit 27 pubs called either the *Cricketers'* or the *Cricketers' Arms*. Cricket was played in Surrey in the 16th century, but the nursery of the modern game was across the border in Hampshire, at a pub now called the *Bat and Ball*, which has become a shrine for devotees of the sport. There were times at this pub when the customers were less respectful. It is said that the house's sixpenny bottles of punch 'would make a cat speak' in those days, and the twopenny pints of beer were 'calculated to put the soul of three butchers into one weaver.' Hampshire has 20 pubs named after the sport which the county helped to nurture, while adjoining Sussex, and Kent, have ten each. Kent also has a *Bat and Ball*, near Sevenoaks – because the pub has given its name to a railway station, it is possible to book a ticket 'to Bat and Ball' – but the county's links with cricket are far more ancient than that.

Cricket, baseball, and even golf, share origins with primitive sports in which participants used a stick to hit a ball, or some less sophisticated missile in the days when a perfect sphere could not be manufactured. One such sport, bat-and-trap, is apparently exclusive to Kent. Bat-and-trap is played primarily at Kent pubs, and especially in Canterbury, where there is a

Rare gathering . . . knur and spel at Upper Barkisland, West Yorkshire, in 1970.

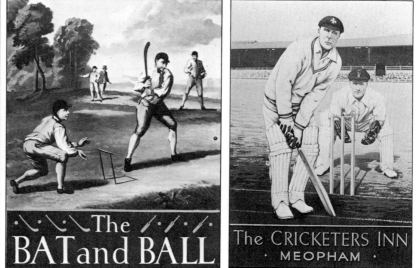

THE SUMMER sport of England was formalized at the Bat and Ball, in Hambledon, Hampshire. The landlord's son, John Nyren, set out the proper playing method in a book called The Young Cricketer's Tutor. Originally, the game was played with a 'crick' (a word meaning a type of stick), as shown on the reverse side of the Bat and Ball's sign. This instrument gave way to the modern bat depicted on the sign of the Cricketers' Inn, at Meopham, Kent. Because the ball frequently passed through the middle of the original double wicket, a third stump was added, so that there could be no doubt when a batsman had been bowled out.

flourishing league; the *Dolphin* and the *Brewer's Delight* are two venues. A similar game, called stoolball, is played in Sussex, usually by women. Although stoolball is not essentially a pub game, it has been known to take place at the *Crown*, in Eastbourne.

The distinguishing feature of bat-and-trap is the fact that the striker himself launches the ball before hitting it. Much the same can be said of tipcat, an improvised game popular with children in the Midlands, and its Cumbrian counterpart of piggy-stick. There is another more formal version of this activity in the North, usually on the Yorkshire side of the Pennines, a pub-based game called knur and spel. Knur derives from the Teutonic word *knorre*, still current in Danish, referring to the knot of applewood which is used as a ball. Spel shares its origins with the modern German and Dutch words *spiel*, meaning 'play.' The knur is hit with a bat called a pommel, which shares its origins with the verb to 'pummel.' Bursts of knur and spel have been known to break out in the Pennines near Halifax: at the *Sportsman*, Midgley, near Hebden Bridge; and the *Spring Rock*, Upper Barkisland. In the same area, a less sophisticated version called billet is played at the *Robin Hood*, Mytholmroyd. The game is also alleged to have taken place occasionally in the area around Barnsley, and further north at the sporting *Tempest Arms*, Elsack, near Skipton.

Such fun should not be allowed to obscure the Yorkshire devotion to cricket (after all, pregnant wives have been dragged across the Pennines so that their anticipated sons would be eligible to play for the right county). There are surprisingly few pubs named after the game in Yorkshire – a mere dozen – but that may be because cricket is considered there to be less of a recreation than a religion.

A pub called the *Yorker* – named after the bowling technique – in Piccadilly, London, is a mini-museum of cricket posters, scorecards and other relics. Sadly, the most famous of

THE WINTER sport of England has traditionally provided a source of licensees for pubs. A retired soccer-player has the celebrity status to attract custom, and a sporting background fits the pub milieu. Once, a footballer retiring in his thirties would be glad to find work as a manager or tenant in a pub. Today's highly-paid professionals sometimes buy their own pubs as a business investment even before they quit playing. Brian Dear (right) played for two London clubs, West Ham and Millwall, before positioning himself behind the bar at the Sorcerer, in Wickford, Essex.

cricket's alcoholically-preserved shrines has now dissolved into a memory. The *Lord's Tavern*, which stood on the boundary line at Lord's – the world's premier cricket ground – was demolished in 1966, just in time to prevent its collapse from sheer old age. The sacrilege of that action is hardly repaired by the new bar which bears its name. The old place may be gone, but a team of sporting and show business celebrities called the Lord's Taverners, who number Prince Charles among past presidents and have his father the Duke of Edinburgh as their '12th man,' still play many matches for charity throughout the season.

Several cricketers have taken pubs on retiring from the game. West Indian Sonny Ramadhin, who was a Lancashire hero, took a pub with his wife – the *White Lion*, on the Yorkshire border at Delph. In the sport-crazy North-East, one brewery alone (Bass Charrington) boasts 25 former athletes among its licensees, including cricketers, footballers, Rugby League players and boxers. In the South, one distinguished drinker and observer of pub life has been heard to complain that every pub on the Brighton road is run by a Second World War fighter-pilot or an ex-Millwall footballer. Whether he is bored with the moustachioed manner of the fighter-pilots, or thinks Millwall a particularly unglamorous football team, is not clear.

Since the maximum pay-level for footballers was abolished, their ambitions upon retirement from the game tend to be more lavish, but there are still a good number of one-time soccer stars behind the bar. One of the best 'locals' in London, the *Thatched House*, in Hammersmith, is splendidly run by ex-England player and former Fulham team manager Bedford Jezzard. His sporting family are true professionals in the pub business, and they are rewarded with a permanently busy house. Few pubs actively involve themselves in football, though the *Stocks*, at Walkden, Manchester, organizes five-a-side soccer.

No sport has more active links with the English pub than

BOXING is the sport most strongly linked with pubs. The boxer on the facing page fought three world title bouts: in California, against Ruben Olivares; in Australia, against Lionel Rose; and in Japan, against Fighting Harada. British, Commonwealth and European bantamweight champion Alan Rudkin became a publican after retiring from the ring, due to injury, while still title-holder. He is pictured at his pub, the Vines, in Liverpool. Rudkin, still a Merseyside hero, is holding his Lonsdale Belt. This trophy, instituted by the boxing patron Lord Lonsdale, is awarded outright to any fighter who has three successful British title bouts in his weight division. Rudkin won five British title fights. He was honoured by the Queen in 1973, with the award of an MBE.

boxing. The relationship stretches back more than 800 years, from the days when inns staged bare-knuckle prize fights in their back-yards, as a regular and money-spinning attraction. The *George*, at Odiham, Hampshire, became a mecca for such contests from its opening in 1547 until the mid-19th century. The action took place in the field behind the building, while the landlord tried to keep pace with the crowd's thirst by serving beer from trestle tables.

The great Tom Sayers was the local hero at the *George*, and he pulled in the crowds for almost 20 years. His career ended on April 17th, 1860, when he fought the young American John Camel Heenan, the 'Benicia Boy,' to a standstill after two epic hours toe-to-toe. Sayers died of brain damage five years later – at the age of 39. Pre-dating Muhammad Ali by more than 100 years, Sayers was also something of a poet, scribbling verses dedicated to his own prowess that were not noted for any false modesty. His 'Farewell to the Ring' still hangs in the *George's* main bar.

Perhaps the best-known pub fighter was Tom Cribb, who himself turned to pulling pints once he had retired from throwing punches. The oddly-named *Ram Jam Inn*, at Stretton, on the Great North Road near Grantham, Lincolnshire, was the scene of his most memorable contest, against the Black American Tom Molyneux, in 1810.

Cribb narrowly won their first bout, but the decision was reversed after allegations that he weighted his punches by holding bullets. The eagerly-awaited return was held at the *Ram Jam*, which also housed both fighters during their preparations. Before a vast crowd, Cribb settled all the arguments by smashing Molyneux's jaw in the eighth round. Two colour prints, produced within five days of the fight, hang today in the *Ram Jam*.

Cribb then retired as 'Champion Boxer of All England' and gentlemen patrons like Lord Byron and William Hazlitt bought him the licence of the *Union Arms* in Panton Street, off the Haymarket in London. He was obviously as popular behind the bar as he was in the ring, for he was a wealthy man by the time he died in 1848. His pub is today largely rebuilt and known in his honour as the *Tom Cribb*, with suitable prints around the walls. The 'jolly dogs' of old Tom's day have been replaced by businessmen grabbing a lunchtime pint, and later in the day by theatre-goers. In 1837 Renton Nicholson penned a few lines to sum up the obviously convivial atmosphere of the pub:

> *Your grog, old boy, is excellent*
> *And nowhere do we meet*
> *More social fun and merriment*
> *Than at yours in Panton Street.*

There are still London boxing pubs which would win the approval both of Nicholson and his jovial host. The best-known

THE NOBLE ART . . . the pugilistic name hardly suited fashionable Hampstead, and now it is called the Load of Hay. The gym remains at this North London house, as it does across the river at the Thomas à Beckett. Both of the capital's famous boxing pubs have been visited by a fistful of world champions.

of these is the *Thomas à Beckett*, in the Old Kent Road. This vast Victorian pub has its own gymnasium and it is here that the top British and visiting boxers, including a whole string of world champions, have trained for their fights in London. It was run by former boxer Tommy Gibbons until his death in 1972, when his widow Beryl took over.

The British Boxing Board of Control has its own gymnasium at the *Load of Hay*, on Haverstock Hill, in Hampstead, London. For many years the pub was known as *The Noble Art*, but for reasons best known to the brewery it has now reverted to its original 18th century name. Perhaps one day it will be renamed the *Muhammad Ali*, for he is a regular visitor when in Britain, holding court while he sips some non-alcoholic beverage.

Much blood has been spilt in the English pub for the entertainment of the customers. But, just as England's history has been a march through bloodshed in the general direction of civilization, so it has been with the pub. Bear-baiting was a popular entertainment in drinking houses, but became largely extinct by the middle of the 19th century. The last great cockfight took place in 1830, at Lincoln, between birds owned by Lord Derby and a breeder named Gilliver. There were seven birds a side, with 1,000 guineas on each individual battle, and 5,000 on the entire match. Gilliver was the winner. Cockfighting has long been illegal, though clandestine meetings still take place in country areas. When the activity was banned, it was widely replaced by another 'blood-sport': Trained dogs were backed to kill a set number of rats in a given time. 'Ratting' was still held at pubs in Birmingham and nearby towns in the early 1900s.

Although the drinking houses of the 18th and 19th centuries were very much the territory of the working classes, 'sporting' events attracted crowds from all sections of society. Not that, in such a rigidly-structured society, the sporting gentlemen who came along, the dandies and toffs, quite condescended to rub shoulders with their less privileged fellows. They were ushered into special seats, well away from the common herd, by the anxious-to-please landlord.

'These have been the resort of hundreds and thousands, from royalty and nobility down to the poorest pauper and the meanest beggar,' reported the London City Mission magazine in 1870, talking of two pubs on London's Battersea fields. 'Surely if ever there was a place out of Hell that surpassed Sodom and Gomorrah in ungodliness and abomination, this was it. Here the worst men and vilest of the human race seem to try to outvie each other in wicked deeds.'

The 'unmentionable doings' at Battersea which scandalized the magazine seemed to include horse-racing, running, betting, fortune-telling, sideshows and 'shameless dancing.' By closing the more conventional places of entertainment, Sabbatarian campaigners had created a gap which publicans with

TOM CRIBB.
CHAMPION OF ENGLAND.
Born at Hanham, Gloucestershire, July 8, 1781.   Height, 5 ft. 10½ in.   Average Weight, 14 st. 3 lb.

Principal Battles.

Beat MADDOX, January 7, 1805.	Beat HORTON, May 10. 1808.
Beat TOM BLAKE, February 15, 1805.	Beat GREGSON, October 25. 1808.
Beat IKEY PIG, May 21, 1805.	Beat JEM BELCHER, February 1, 1809.
Beaten by GEORGE NICHOLLS, July 20, 1805.	Beat MOLINEAUX, December 10, 1810.
Beat BILL RICHMOND, October 8, 1805.	Beat MOLINEAUX, September 28, 1811.
Beat JEM BELCHER, April 8, 1807.	Beat CARTER (room turn up), February 1, 1820.

ENGLISH CHAMPION Tom Cribb, a barefisted prize-fighter, is honoured by a pub at the heart of London's West End. It's hardly a sporting pub, though he was once the landlord. Today, its origins are recalled in sporting prints around the walls.

available land gratefully filled by organizing 'Sunday fairs.' For a time, London pubs which had their own grounds inventively ran 'pleasure gardens', until the city grew outwards and swallowed them up. As society groped its way towards civilization, blood-sports met with a growing public revulsion. Temperance activity in the early 20th century toned-down sporting entertainments in pubs, while cities began to develop a wider range of facilities for leisure.

In modern times, the strongest reminder of the pub's connection with blood-sports is the fox-hunt, meeting outside a country inn for a stirrup-cup before setting out. In the great hunting shires of Northampton and Leicester – the latter including the old county of Rutland, with its fine beer – this characteristically English sight can be seen most winter weekends. Elsewhere in England, hunts meet in places as far apart as the *Cat and Fiddle*, at Exeter, and the *Blue Cap*, in Sandiway, Cheshire. In John Peel's Cumbrian countryside, the bloodless sport of hound-trailing is also popular. The dogs follow an aniseed trail, and a system of handicapping and timing decides the winner. At the *Red Lion*, near Ulverston, the hounds are actually kept on the premises.

The throwing of horse-shoes on to a hook or stick as a casual game gave rise to what was once a major English sport, quoits. In some parts of the country, this game still takes place, employing considerable skills, subtle tactics, and very heavy quoits. It also continues to be played in one or two places with horseshoes (the original game was equally popular in The Netherlands, when it was transplanted to the United States and South Africa). The landlord of the appropriately-named *Horse and Groom*, at Wivenhoe, near Colchester, has made some claims to be a champion with the shoes. The term 'shoes' is also used to indicate the actual quoits in the more formal version of the game, which is played over an 18-yard pitch in East Anglian pubs. There are leagues at Hadleigh and Rougham, in Suffolk, and the game has a stronghold at the *Angel*, at Braintree, Essex. East Anglia also has a form of indoor quoits, called caves. This version of the game appears to be in a state of decline, though the small town of Bury St. Edmunds can claim a couple of pubs with caves, the *Black Boy*, and the *Shepherd and Dog*. In the West of England, outdoor quoits has been revived at the *Tyning Inn*, Radstock, between Bath and Wells, and the Vale of Evesham has a miniature version called dobbers. The most serious and skilful quoiting is in the North-East, where the sport is played over an 11-yard pitch by shipyard workers and miners, as well as farm folk, with betting on games. The technical terms are elaborate, as explained in an article by the distinguished writer Paul Jennings: 'You score a point with a ringer, but here again the skill lies in shots with names like pot, back pot, hill-gater, Frenchman, in which the quoit lies in a position making it impossible for anyone else to get a ringer.' In North Yorkshire, quoit-players like to take a run-up of two or three yards, before throwing underarm with the right hand. In County Durham and Northumberland, a crouching, back-hand lob is favoured. Northern quoits are

RATTING . . . faced by a dog which has been trained to kill them as quickly as possible, the rats scurry hopelessly into corners. This engraving of a bloody scene at the long-gone Graham Arms was an illustration in the investigative work London Labour and the London Poor, by Henry Mayhew. The famous report on social conditions in the capital was published in 1851. Mayhew, apart from being a crusading journalist and lawyer, was one of the founders of the then-satirical magazine Punch.

THE HUNT MEETS at a remote country inn, to the South of Shrewsbury, and not far from the Welsh border. The inn is named the Stiperstones after the hills which form its backdrop. Hunt meetings at the inn are sporadic, but there are said to be gatherings of a different sort on the rocky Stiperstones each year on Midwinter's Night. Legend has it that devils gather there to choose their leader. To the East of these rocks is the Long Mynd, a ten-mile ridge of hills, with an ancient track running the length of its crest.

played at the *Plough*, Sleights, hear Whitby, Yorkshire; the *Three Tuns*, Birtley, County Durham; and the *Wheatsheaf*, Corbridge, Northumberland, among other places. (A more recent recreation at the *Three Tuns* is the bizarre Northern sport of welliehoying. The object is to see who can throw farthest a Wellington boot.)

An endless variety of pastimes has been improvised and evolved to test the bizarre skills of drinking men, and every game exists in a range of local versions. Such fecklessness was a cause of concern to a whole series of kings, who banned seemingly-innocent games on pain of serious fines. Quoits was made illegal by Richard II, and players were taken to court, but James I and Charles I emerged as friends of the game. This odd and lasting form of oppression was not without reason. Edward III took a particularly hard line over games, and demanded that sporting

ROBIN HOOD, 13th-century archer, outlaw, and the Sheriff of Nottingham's greatest adversary, is celebrated in that city by a fine local pale ale. A lesser-known hero of the same period, also a bowman, is remembered in one of the beers of Greater Manchester. The original Middleton Archer was probably Edmund Plantagenet, Duke of Lancaster, a left-handed bowman whose courageous leadership saved the township of Middleton during a particularly hard battle. A subsequent local devotion to bowmanship reputedly took Middleton Archers to Crécy, Agincourt and Flodden, and is still recalled by the local brand of stout. The local brewer, John Willie Lees, has a pub in the town-centre of Middleton called the Archer.

activity be restricted to such martial arts as archery. The long-bow, a difficult but potent weapon, was unique to the British Isles. Even at the peak of England's military success with the bow, Edward was concerned that his subjects should keep their skills well sharpened. There are still pubs with archery grounds, including the *Abbey*, at St. John's Wood, London.

However, when today's drinkers talk about arrows, they are more likely to mean darts. It was from archery that darts sprang, and became the most popular of all pub games. Although the original dartboards were improvised from the ends of wine butts, a more formal game had already begun to emerge by the turn of the 17th century. As its military origins grew more remote, the darts themselves became slighter.

Even in its modern tidy form, a game of darts takes space and time, and the sport hasn't always been popular with profit-crazed brewery managements. Nonetheless, most 'locals' have retained their dartboards, even if they are often restricted to the public (ie working-class) bars. The *Castle*, at Tooting, in London, has a dozen boards. There are a million registered players, taking part with some seriousness in winter league matches between pubs in their towns, and at least six times as many occasional dart-throwers. The Pilgrim Fathers may not have been ideal material for the English pub darts team, but they still played on their journey to the New World. The game was exported for a second time by British-based American Service-men after World War II; Generals Eisenhower and Patton are recalled as enthusiastic players at the *Bells*, in Lower Peover, Cheshire.

Although the standard English game is based on a scoring system which descends from a 301-point start, there are many variations. It is possible to start with 401, 501 or even 1,001 points, or to adopt an entirely different set of rules while using a standard board, in games like 'Killer,' 'Shanghai,' or 'Cricket.' There are also regional variations employing boards which are marked in different ways.

East End darts is a fine example. It is a form of the game confined to Cockney territory, within the sound of Bow Bells, except for an odd outpost at Ipswich, Suffolk. The game is so local that few outsiders, even lifelong Londoners, are aware that it exists. It employs a board split into only 12 sections, repeating the numbers 5, 15, 10, 20. The doubles and trebles rings are much narrower than on the standard board. The *Resolute*, in Poplar High Street, has been a stronghold of the East End game, along with the *Old Star*, in Wapping, the *Duke of Wellington*, in Bow, and the *Queen's Head*, in Stepney.

Yorkshire darts uses a standard-size board, without a treble ring or outer bull. It is not widely played in the county, but has flourished in the *Tempest Arms*, a sporting pub at Elsack, near Skipton. Across the Pennines things are, of course, completely

ARROWS are still called for in pubs, though the word may be enunciated as 'arrers,' and the missiles proffered may be small enough to throw at a dartboard. Years of pride and practice in archery passed on to the more compact contest with darts. Since only one person can throw at a time, darts as a team sport has a quality which sustains the popularity of any pub game; there is plenty of time for drinking between plays. The darts match above, with the names of each team's players chalked on the score-board, took place at a pub called the Wonder, in the London suburb of Enfield.

different. Lancashire darts is played on much smaller boards, which are traditionally soaked in beer. The numbering is in a different sequence, there are no trebles and only a very narrow doubles ring. This unusual game has long-standing links with *The Old House at Home*, at Withington, Manchester. One of the most ancient variations is played at many pubs in the brewing town of Burton-on-Trent. There are no outer bull or trebles, and two small, 25-point squares are placed to the left and right of the boards. They are, however, known as 'practice boards' by the locals, who play on them mainly for the sake of tradition, and stick to the standard game in competition.

The only game that comes anywhere near to rivalling darts on a national scale is dominoes. Although the game was played by the Ancient Chinese, and spread into Europe via Italy, it was not introduced to Britain until French prisoners-of-war in Napoleonic times were seen to play it. One explanation for the name of the game attributes it to the Italian domino hood, first worn by churchmen, then adapted as an evening veil for masquerade balls. The idea is that the blackness of the dominoes and the concealment essential to the game suggested the metaphorical name. An alternative theory is that the winner might have cried *faire domino!* The French still say *faire capot!* In its early days in England, dominoes was confined to the working-classes; cards was thought a more proper pastime for gentlemen. Dominoes is still a working-class game, but its popularity is immense; card-games like cribbage are still played in pubs on a very small scale,

but the law limits gambling on such games to very small stakes. Although dominoes can easily be learned from anyone who plays, the experts develop their skills to a daunting level. In the basic game, each player has a set number of pieces (usually six or seven). The players then put pieces down alternately, always matching their dominoes with one already on the table which has the same number of white spots in its markings. In a simple game, the winner would be the first person to get rid of all his pieces, but the skill lies in reducing as quickly as possible the numerical value of your pieces, while deducing and memorizing the contents of your opponent's hand.

A much older game which still enjoys great popularity is shove ha'penny. This game has had an important part in English

DOMINOES, like darts, can be played either informally or in organized tournaments. Lots of pubs keep sets of darts and dominoes behind the bar to be used by customers. These are overwhelmingly the most popular pub games, each played everywhere in England, but there are still geographical differences in emphasis. While working-class pubs in London would yield to none in their devotion to darts, the North's competitive sporting inclinations make for a more earnest attitude towards dominoes. The North-Eastern interlude above was captured at the Albion, Sunderland.

recreation, under a variety of names. Henry VIII was an enthusiastic but erratic player, and his regular losses sent a ripple of scandal through the court. The records of the Privy Purse for 1532 show: 'Lord William won 9L (pounds) of the King at Shovilla Bourde.' On the credit side, it went on to reveal that His Majesty took £45 from Lord Rochforde in his next game. In the early days some 'shuffle boards' were sometimes ten yards long, and saucer-sized discs were used. Joseph Strutt, author of *Sports and Pastimes* writes in 1801 of having seen 'in a low public house in Benjamin Street, near Clerkenwell Green, a board which is about three feet in breadth and thirty-nine feet two inches in length, and said to be far the largest of its kind in London.'

Today's standard board is about 18 inches long and, as it was 400 years ago, is divided into nine parallel sections, the 'beds.' The object is to flick five halfpennies, or polished metal discs, with the heel of the hand into each bed in turn. The composition of the board itself differs up and down the country. Northern boards tend to be of polished hardwood, which needs much devotion to keep it in condition. In the South and West, slate boards, slicked with French chalk, are standard. Hampshire is keen shove ha'penny country, with two particularly splendid boards at the *Cat and Fiddle*, a picturesque inn on the edge of the New Forest, between Christchurch and Ringwood. In Dorset, the Isle of Purbeck has its own local version of the game, played with Guernsey halfpennies. When the Isle of Purbeck was more isolated than it is today, its fishermen knew St. Peter Port, Guernsey, as well as they knew any town. Another very narrowly localized version is push-penny, played in Stamford, Lincolnshire. This game is played with only three coins, usually Queen Victoria 'bun' pennies.

Board games like draughts, and even backgammon, are not unknown in pubs. Another Eastern game, dating back to about 1370 BC, was brought by the invading Normans. The game is sometimes known as Nine Men's Morris (perhaps a corruption of Moorish, as it was in 'Morris Dancing'). Another name is merels, based on the Latin 'merellus,' for a token or counter; there are dozens of local corruptions and variations in England. Merels is a board game rather like a sophisticated and mobile form of noughts-and-crosses. It has been seen at several pubs in different parts of the country, including three at Stratford-on-Avon: the *Bell Inn*, Shottery; the *Black Swan*; and the *Alveston Manor Hotel*. There are also one or two dice games, a very simple form of roulette, games in which coins or weights are tossed into holes (one version is called toad-in-the-hole), and a sport in which a ring attached to a halter is thrown on to a bull's horn. (The horn has first been removed from the bull, and fixed on the wall of the pub.)

The American sport of bowling has its origins in the family of games which includes skittles and English bowls. This in-

CUSTOMS which might otherwise wither in the climate of the mid 20th century need the protection which can be offered by the pub. Games which require neither hyperbolical media coverage nor expensive facilities can find a social context in the local. An improvised sport can gain popularity and develop its own form, sometimes determinedly local, sometimes national. Perhaps off-duty warriors once put their clubs to peaceful use in a game like the ancient Cornish sport of keels, pictured below. From such a simple concept emerged several distinct local versions of skittles, the American tenpin game, and English bowls. Another game deeply rooted in pub culture, with occasional local variations, is shove ha'penny. The game thrives now as it did when the picture on the right was taken in a London pub during the 1950s.

The law provides for betting on a limited scale on games like cribbage, pictured on the far right in the North-East during the 1970s.

terbred family is full of local idiosyncrasies, and it has taken a son of Ireland, Timothy Finn, to track down almost a dozen examples in his delightful and informative work *Pub Games of England.*

The popular reputation of skittles as a West Country sport is borne out by its predominant position among pub pastimes there, but variations of the game exist all over the Southern half of England. Even within each style of skittles, there are often several different ways of playing. The principal style of skittles – which involves rolling or pitching balls down an alley at nine or ten pins – is played in all those counties which could even remotely be described as being in the Western part of England. 'Western skittles' is particularly popular in Dorset (which has several versions, including one called 'Puddletown Rules'), Wiltshire, Gloucestershire, the county of Avon (perhaps the game's strongest area, with the pitching method popular in the city of Bath), Somerset and Devon. A similar style, called 'Old English,' was once a London sport, and is still played in a handful of pubs there. This is the most strenuous form of skittles, played with a heavy discus called a 'cheese.' 'Old English skittles' is still played at the *Duke's Head,* in Lower Richmond Road, Putney, and the *Freemasons' Arms,* on Downshire Hill, Hampstead. The latter pub also has an ancient form of lawn billiards, called mell, and sometimes known as pell-mell, among other spellings. The expression 'pell-mell' meaning fast, and the place-name Pall Mall, both originate from this game. (A variety of more conventional billiards and pool games are also played in pubs.) The area around the city of Oxford has a variation on skittles called 'Aunt Sally,' in which sticks are thrown at a 'doll.' This outdoor game is organized on a formal league basis. Further north, but still among the Midland counties, Leicestershire and Nottinghamshire have a bouncing style of 'long alley' skittles.

Leicestershire also plays a type of 'Hood Skittles,' one of several miniature versions of the game, though the original form is in neighbouring Northamptonshire. The crafts of Northampton's leather industry presumably spawned the elaborate upholstered table that is used in this much-loved indoor game. Even more miniaturized styles used to exist further East, in Norfolk and Kent. Timothy Finn reports rare sightings of 'Norfolk skittles' at the *Horseshoes,* near Erpingham, and Kent 'daddlums' at the *Vigo Inn,* near Meopham. A tiny bagatelle style of skittles was once played under the name of 'Dorset table,' and a board can still be found at the *King's Arms,* Portesham, in that county. A miniature version called 'roly poly' seems to be extinct, but 'Devil among the tailors' is still played all over the Southern half of England, albeit on a small scale. This game, which uses a ball on a string, was invented in London. One pub there which has a table is the *Crabtree,* in Rainville Road, Fulham.

The English game of bowls is known to every schoolboy as

CROWN-GREEN bowling is most likely to be seen in the North, especially Lancashire. One of the most important pub venues is the Waterloo Hotel (facing page), in Blackpool.

the sport which was being played on Plymouth Hoe when the Spanish Armada approached. Sir Francis Drake is said to have insisted on finishing his game before leading the English force which repelled the would-be invaders. At that time, it is likely that the difference between games in which balls are bowled at skittles and games in which they are bowled at another ball had not yet been formalized. Today, the game of bowls is a highly-organized summer sport played all over England, and a good number of pubs have their own carefully-manicured greens. The best-known version of the game is played on a flat green, but Northerners prefer a more sophisticated style employing a green which rises gently to a barely-perceptible 'crown.'

Land prices have tended to prohibit greens at today's London pubs, but there are still several in suburban areas. Examples are the *Old Cherry Tree*, at Southgate, and the *Olde Harrow*, at Thames Ditton. In the West Midlands, the *Bell*, at Halford, near Moreton-in-the-Marsh, Gloucestershire, is a pleasant bowls pub. East Anglia is a particularly strong area for flat-green bowling, at pubs like the *White Horse*, Badington, Suffolk; the *Royal Oak*, Godmanchester, Cambridgeshire; the *Hatchet and Bill*, Yakley, Peterborough; and the *Mail Cart*, Spalding, Lincolnshire. The history of crown-green bowling is even more closely linked with drinking-houses, though the most important venues do not allow drinks to be brought near the precious turf. The popularity of crown-green bowling starts in the West Midlands, reaches its peak in the North-West (Lancashire and Cheshire), then crosses the Pennines. Apart from being the more interesting game, it offers the bonus of some fine Northern beers. Among the breweries owning Northern bowling pubs are Marston, Evershed; Greenall, Whitley; Burtonwood; Boddington; and Mitchells of Lancaster. Notable bowling pubs in the North-West include the *Brown Edge Vaults*, in the Rugby League town of St. Helens; the *Waterloo*, in Blackpool, the

THE BILLIARDS family of games makes the odd appearance in pubs, but today's houses are unlikely to be as well-appointed as the 1890s venue above. Eight-ball pool was a 1970s innovation. The game on the right was at the Wheatsheaf, a pub with a colourful clientele, in Hammersmith, London.

WHAT HAPPENS WHEN ENGLAND GETS MERRIE

The oddball games of England are countless. The Haxey Hood Game, pictured on the immediate right, is played in Lincolnshire on Twelfth Night (January 6). First, there is a pub-to-pub procession, with songs like John Barleycorn. Then the residents of Haxey and nearby towns form themselves into two teams of indeterminate size and, led by characters in curious costume, scramble for several hours after a ceremonial leather hood. The side who can first get the hood into a local pub are rewarded with free beer. Collections are held in pubs in order to pay for damage caused by the game. Equally strange pursuits such as rhubarb-thrashing (far right) and marrow-dangling (below) are invested with origins deep in local folklore by drinkers at the Greyhound, Wargrave-on-Thames. Such sentiments, like the 'games' themselves, testify to the strength of good beer.

North's most famous seaside resort; and the *Boot and Shoe*, in Lancaster, which has two greens.

A third style of bowls, the French game of *petanque*, has crossed the Channel and found a home in the Southern counties. In the South-East, *petanque* is played at several Essex pubs, notably in Braintree and Rayne. The English headquarters of the game are alleged to be at Shedfield, Southampton, at *Sam's Hotel*.

There is no limit to the Englishman's imagination when he has had a few beers, as evidenced by the pastimes which have been devised in pubs. Much controversy surrounds, for example, the origins of dwyle-flunking (or flonking). Sceptics assert strongly that it was invented in a bizarre television comedy show in the 1960s, and that life has imitated art. Others are convinced that the television show was merely satirizing a time-honoured game which was once the court pastime of King Offa of Mercia. The Mercian connection is questionable, since that kingdom was centred in the West Midlands, and dwyle-flunking takes place mainly in the East. It is interesting to note, though, that *dwiel* is a Dutch word for a dish-cloth, and The Netherlands have played a big part in the history of Eastern England.

In the television version, the dwyle, a rag or mophead soaked in stale beer, was used by a 'batsman' to hit, or 'flunk,' 'fielders,' who joined hands in a circle around him. This esoteric pastime has been seen at the *Farmer's Boy*, Kensworth, Bedfordshire, the *Old Ox*, Shillingstone, Dorset, and the *Woolpack*, Ipswich, Suffolk. A second, allegedly ancient, version of the game has the two teams meeting halfway between their respective pubs. Each is armed with a stick and the object is to knock a rag ball, soaked in beer, through the front door of the opposing pub. The losers must buy beer for the rest of the day.

If that seems a little too sedate, rhubarb-thrashing may be the answer. This supposedly age-old game has been played at the *Greyhound*, Wargrave-on-Thames, Berkshire. It involves two blindfold players who stand in dustbins, grasping each other by the left arm and thrashing each other with sticks of rhubarb until one is driven from his bin.

The same pub has staged marrow dangling, in which a marrow (out of season, anything resembling one will do) is hung by string from an upright pole. One team stands in a circle with buckets on their heads. The marrow is swung by opposing team members in turn. Points are scored for every bucket – or opponent – who is knocked over.

Some houses belonging to Workington Brewery, in Cumbria, play a game called egg-dumping. Eggs are knocked together, and the last survivor wins. The same brewery has pubs in the town of Wigton which take part in general-knowledge quizzes on a league basis.

Life has its serious moments, even in the English pub.

Singing and Dancing
The arts and the pub

THE THREAD of continuity is homespun entertainment. The singing may be impromptu or organized, solo or ensemble. The dancing is emphatically informal. Singing at the Derby Arms, a suburban London pub at Sheen, near Richmond (left). Dancing in the North-East of England, at the Albion, Sunderland (above).

THERE HAVE BEEN pub singsongs since the Anglo-Saxons 'wassailed' in their ale-houses; Shakespeare performed at inns; the music-hall was born in the Victorian public house; English pop-music has origins in the pub; and the London theatre's fringe is there, too. Although the overwhelming majority of houses eschew anything louder than conversation and drinking, the performing arts nonetheless owe a huge and continued debt to the English pub.

There are pubs enough where the best-projected sound is that of the local bore, and pubs which quite properly cater for the puritanical English love of lugubriousness, but there are also country pubs in Cornish and Suffolk coastal villages and Yorkshire valleys where fine voices are a part of the folk-culture. There are urban locals where the uniquely-jangling pub piano has not yet surrendered to the jukebox, and where an impromptu singsong can break out if that is the mood of the house. There are pubs with a drum-kit in the corner, or a tiny stage, where local musicians may play once a week. There are pubs that specialize in entertainment: from music-hall revivals to 'drag' or strip-shows; from Irish bands to country-and-western; folk music to Black British reggae; New Orleans music to contemporary jazz. There are pubs with a permanent theatre bar, pubs featuring the occasional poetry-reading, pubs that from time to time act as art-galleries.

The thread of continuity has been the singsong. The Saxons had round-songs that were passed from singer to singer with each new verse; the strolling players of Shakespeare's time performed for an audience; the Victorians of London's East End echoed the music-hall with their own vocal 'knees-up.'

Medieval minstrels were expected not just to sing for their supper, but to tell tales, too. At a time when communications were poor, strolling players arriving at a wayside inn quickly gathered a crowd, eager for their gossip, badinage and ill-

THE JUKE-BOX made an early entry, before the turn of the century: advertisement from the Licensed Victuallers' Gazette. The disco-pub arrived in the 1960s, but live music still thrives. A bizarre assortment of entertainments (facing page) at a pub in a working-class district of London, between Camden Town and Holloway. Country music is popular among the large local Irish population.

informed political opinion. In coaching days, North and South-bound mails often coincided at Stony Stratford, in Buckinghamshire, where the two inns were the *Cock* and *Bull*. Passengers exchanged tattle in the two inns, muddling and exaggerating accounts of what was afoot in the country. Tales emanating from Stony Stratford always seemed difficult to believe, and they became known as 'Cock and Bull stories.'

The exchange of rhetoric was for several centuries organized into formal contests. The opponents would face each other across the room at an inn and, instead of having a fist-fight, would trade witty insults. The contest lasted for a pre-arranged time, with a referee to decide who had won, though either contestant could be disqualified for losing his temper. The 17th-century low-lifer Ned Ward reported in his publication *London Spy* that he came across such a contest at a pub in Billingsgate, near the fish market. At the end of a narrow lane stinking of 'stale sprats and piss,' he found a pub full of fishwives whose 'cheeks were as plump as an infant's arse.' As Ned entered, one large lady drew herself up and volleyed at her opponent: 'You white-livered son of a Fleet Street bum-seller! I know your kind, begot in a sedan-chair at noon between Ludgate Hill and Temple Bar. Who are you calling a whore? I'm not like the mangy street-walker who brought you into the world, and I wouldn't waste my piss on you if you fell into the fire!'

The game was called flighting. Dr Johnson, who favoured such Fleet Street pubs as the *Cheshire Cheese*, the *Cock* and the *Mitre*, is said to have been flighting when he produced the line: 'Sir, your wife, under the pretext of keeping a bawdy house, is, in fact, the receiver of stolen goods.' Karl Marx is reputed to have involved himself in this sort of thing at the *Museum Tavern*, in Bloomsbury, across the road from the scene of his studies. A 'flighting' event was more recently organized there between Brendan Behan's brother Brian (a well-known political activist), and an Irish peer.

Words and music filled England's inns often enough through their history, and set the stage for drama. But drama made a late entrance.

The public's experience of drama in the early Middle Ages rarely extended beyond miracle plays and morality plays in the town square. Theatrical troupes performed only in the banqueting halls of country houses and castles until the beginnings of the Renaissance, and the subsequent flowering of English literature. Managers of troupes then began to experiment by taking their shows on the road, and the yards of inns provided the logical place in which to perform. Profit-conscious landlords soon built galleries from which their customers could get a better view, and very occasionally tented-over the yard to keep out the weather.

The era of Shakespeare, Ben Jonson and Marlowe saw many inns given over entirely to the theatre, in much the way

FOR YOUR ENTERTAINMENT.

MON: WHITE WITCH. D.J.
DISCO. & TOPLESS GO-GO.

TUES: ROCK NIGHT WITH.....
LITTLE ARTHUR.

WED: DISCO. D.J. RICKY
FRANCIS. ALSO TOPLESS GO-GO.

THURS: COUNTRY &
WESTERN NIGHT.
THE SHEVA GROUP.

FRI: & SAT: JACK &
THE CRICKLEWOOD GREEN.

SUN: THE WASHALLS
WITH POP-HARMONEY.

GOOD
COMPANY.
GOOD SERVICE.
AND TRUMAN
FOR REALLY
PARTICULAR
HU...

THE
BRECKNOCK

THE HALLS were a phenomenon of the late 1800s, though the one established by Sam Collins (top) had an astonishingly long life. 'Collins' Music Hall,' in Islington, London, survived cinema, radio and TV only to close in its centenary year of 1962 – on the eve of a revival in music-hall. The most famous artist of the halls was Marie Lloyd, pictured above for an article in the Licensed Victuallers' Gazette of 1898. Music as the Universal Language of Mankind is captured in rich colour by a window (facing page) at the pub, opposite Liverpool's concert hall.

modern pubs are sometimes turned into discos. The bars and eating-halls became ancillary to the acting area. Five major London inns of the late 16th century became essentially licensed theatres: the *Boar's Head*, at Whitechapel; the *Bell Sauvage*, on Ludgate Hill; and the *Bull, Cross Keyes* and *Bell*, all in Grace-church Street. The *Bell Sauvage* seemed to be cursed: several actors died while on stage there, and the devil himself was said to have appeared in a puff of brimstone and smoke during a performance of Marlowe's *Faust*. Marlowe and Shakespeare used to drink at the *Mermaid*, but it is the *George*, in Southwark, which survives as the strongest reminder of the period. Outside of London, the *New Inn*, at Gloucester, is perhaps the best preserved galleried inn.

The fatal problem with galleried inns lay in making sure that each member of the audience paid for the entertainment, and it was as a result of this difficulty that theatres like the Globe – Shakespeare's 'wooden "O"' – were constructed. These were purpose-built theatres, copying the style of the galleried inns, but with a fixed pay-box through which patrons had to enter. The inn had spawned the theatre.

The two institutions have retained a colourful relationship over the years, never more so than when brewer and Member of Parliament Samuel Whitbread raised £400,000 to rebuild the *Theatre Royal*, Drury Lane, in 1812, after it had been destroyed by fire. The initiative for Whitbread's involvement came from the playright Sheridan, who had been the principal financial victim of the Drury Lane fire. Sheridan, who was also an MP, had run the theatre as a source of income to support his political career, an intention which was constantly thwarted by his in-ability to manage money.

A night at the theatre in those days was rounded-off with a visit to a 'supper room' or 'music room.' Every other street-corner had one; they were drinking houses which had adapted to the needs of the times. Customers were en-couraged to 'get up from the floor' and provide their own entertainment by singing or reciting. In some of these places, poets bravely declaimed their verses, a practice which met with the disapproval of Lord Byron in *English Bards and Scottish Reviewers*. By and large, the gentry who went 'slumming' in music rooms liked either vulgarity or bathos with their post-theatre drink; dirty songs and tear-jerking ballads became the general rule.

The mixture was ignited by the landlord of Lambeth's *Canterbury Arms*, Charles Morton, who first added two important elements: in place of amateurs 'from the floor,' he hired pro-fessional or semi-pro entertainers, and he built on to his house a room with a stage. His house was packed every night, and Morton is now recognized as the father of music hall.

The music-hall's heyday was the second half of the 19th

Music
is the
Universal
Language
of
Mankind
Longfellow

THE BIRTH OF THE HALLS

The Melody lingers on: an informal singsong at the Drury Tavern, in London's Strand (1), and the more formal concert-room with entertainment by a 'harmonic assembly,' at the Three Tuns, Fetter Lane (2), in 1835. In such concert-rooms, local talent was gradually replaced by professional performers. Later, proper stages were built in bar-parlours, like the one at the Borough Music Hall, in Southwark (3), of 1859. The Surrey 'Music Hall' (4) had pioneered the new terminology in 1848, and there were soon enough such places to be advertised in 'What's On' publications like Paul Pry (5). Eventually, pubs began to build extensions to house their music-hall entertainment. The large hall added to Deacon's, in Clerkenwell (6), in 1861, was typical. Music-hall ultimately gave way to variety (vaudeville), but the 'original' style enjoyed its novelty revival in the 1960s, and a version persisted in the mid-1970s at the Pindar of Wakefield, Gray's Inn Road (7).

A view of Deacon's Music Hall which was demolished in 1891 for the making of Rosebery Avenue.

THE LORD NELSON TAVERN.

century, when England's cities were doubling and trebling in population as a consequence of industrial growth. There were audiences enough for performances throughout the week and, because the performers came out every night, they were described as 'stars.' It is not certain who coined the term, though it has been credited to publican Morton, but 'stars' were to shine in American vaudeville and later in Hollywood. The music-hall stars were badly paid, with occasional exceptions like Vesta Tilley and Marie Lloyd, and many of them died young.

The pub's role in presenting music-hall entertainment followed the precedent set by the Shakespearean theatre: once the institution grew up, it broke away to find a separate existence. Lavish music halls, as ornate as 'legitimate' theatres, were built by entrepreneurs like Stoll and Moss, who also used their influence – in conjunction with the more sober citizens – to discourage the pubs from presenting such entertainment.

Only the pub piano, and regulars' occasional 'knees-up,' remained to recall that period. In the first half of the 20th century, the pub was afflicted by the temperance movement and the restrictive legislation which followed, and by the economic consequences of two world wars. As a focal point for public morale, the pub played a vital role, but its expressive vigour was damped for decades.

A bizarre sign of revival in the 1940s had a lasting effect in popular music, and said something for the resilience of the pub as a cultural seed-bed. A British trumpeter, George Webb, tried with a few friends to re-create the jazz idiom of New Orleans in his local pub, the *Red Barn*, at Bexleyheath, near London. This esoteric exercise attracted young musicians from all over London, many of whom later became respected names in British jazz. The movement eventually permeated British popular music, creating an astonishing and money-spinning boom in 'traditional jazz' throughout Europe during the 1950s. Many of the 'trad' bands followed the example of George Webb (who himself gained neither wealth nor fame from the fashion), and played in pubs. Long after the boom ended, a strong strain of jazz persisted in a great many pubs. Several jazz pubs became famous for the visiting American musicians whom they featured, notably the *Bull's Head*, an attractive old house in the London 'village' of Barnes. Among the musicians to have appeared there are Zoot Sims, such veterans as Jimmy Witherspoon and the late Ben Webster, and the folk singer Joan Baez.

An even more incongruous spin-off from the jazz boom started the British invasion of the American record charts. Traditional jazz had a subsidiary movement called 'skiffle,' derived from the 'rent party' music of the American Blacks. Its chief exponent was the son-in-law of a publican from the Limehouse district of London. He took his name from the American blues-shouter Lonnie Johnson, borrowed a song from Leadbelly, and

A handful of pubs play host to brass bands . . . performance in the yard of the Black Swan, at Helmsley, a market town in the North York Mo

made a hit. 'Lonnie' Donegan's *Rock Island Line* was the first British record to sell a million in the United States. It paved the way for later British musicians like the Rolling Stones, who were 'discovered' playing in the Railway Hotel, at Richmond, near London. Rock'n'roll, too, has a place in the English pub.

The most surprising of all the modern entertainment phenomena in pubs owes much to TV journalist Dan Farson, son of the American author Negley Farson. Long before nostalgia became fashionable, he bought a run-down pub in London's East End and set out to re-create the music hall. For a time, in the mid-1960s, ventures like Farson's were a great success. He believes they worked because they offered, 'instead of synthetic transatlantic performers, which were fashionable then,' people like Tommy Pudding ('Put a bit of Treacle on your Pudding, Mary Anne'), Mrs Shufflewick, Ida Barr in her eighties, a taxi-driver who sang Jolson songs, and 'a girl who was known as the white mouse, so startlingly off-key that she was greeted with cheers whenever she appeared.' They were not, as Farson points out, 'false stars.'

Judy Garland once leaped on to the stage at Farson's *Waterman's Arms*, and held an audience of brown-ale drinkers spellbound with a performance of *Come Rain, Come Shine*, accompanied only by the pub piano. Eventually, the music-hall revival faded away. Farson left the *Waterman's*; Queenie Watts left another great East End entertainment pub, the *Iron Bridge*; but a strand had been woven into the pub culture. They still have music-hall nights at one or two houses, and they are an established part of the pub repertoire.

What happened to the boom? Once again, the amateurs were pushed out by professionals, and the whole business gained a commercial intensity. Topless dancers and striptease took over. The only 'burlesque' element to retain a fashionability was 'drag,' a term which dates back to Georgian London. In Georgian days, both performers and audience dressed in drag – men as women, and women as men – and the question of the day was, 'tell me, pretty hobbledehoy are you girl or are you boy?' A good number of Georgian taverns were hobbledehoy houses, and one of their most famous habitues was an apparent hermaphrodite who went by the name of the Chevalier D'Eon. The Chevalier wore long skirts and ballgowns, and fought all-comers with a rapier for money.

Transvestites in Georgian taverns were not necessarily homosexual, and the same is true today. Drag artists are drawn from all sorts of situations, though a growing number are professional actors. A London showbusiness writer who studied the phenomenon of drag estimated that not more than 20 per cent of performers were homosexual. 'Although the audiences obviously include a fair number of overt gays, drag is principally popular in pubs which attract married couples rather than single men.

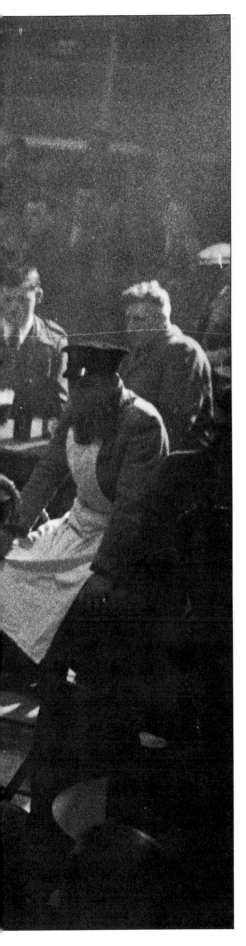

For some reason, women tend to be the most avid fans. In the big London drag pubs like the *Black Cap*, in Camden Town, and the *Cricketers'*, at Battersea, the atmosphere tends to be comic. The performers play for laughs – there is nothing particularly sexual about drag.'

Those music-hall pubs which were not subsequently caught up in the drag craze often tried straight theatre as an alternative. This enjoyed some popularity in the late 1960s, and settled down to become a regular feature of the fringe theatre in the 1970s. Of the half-dozen theatre pubs in London, two achieved something of a reputation: the *Bush*, at Shepherd's Bush; and the *King's Head*, in Islington.

The *King's Head* became a theatre-pub when ex-actor Dan Crawford took over as landlord. International names like John Hurt and Janet Suzman have played there, as well as many student actors. Productions have been a mix of established works and new plays, and the Arts Council of Great Britain has provided limited financial help. Most of the cost has been met by box-office takings, the bar and the serving of meals. The *King's Head* has also presented folk-music concerts and poetry-readings.

Unlike the *King's Head*, the Taverners drama group frowned upon drinking during performances, and that undoubtedly contributed to their demise as a pioneering force. The Taverners, with a repertoire including Chekhov, Galsworthy, Shaw and Sheridan, were formed in 1937, after a letter appealing for support had been published in *The Times* over a list of prominent signatures. They gave more than 50 performances, including 15 plays and poetry-reading sessions, before the war. *The Times*

STRIP ACTS like the one on the left blossomed in the 1950s. Pubs promoted such attractions to dissuade their customers from staying at home in the evenings . . . television was spreading fast. Ironically, pub 'cabaret' was so successful that it was aped by a popular TV series during the early 1960s. And TV presenter Dan Farson completed the circle by running a pub, the Waterman's Arms (above).

*ARE YOU girl or are you boy?
Drag artist (previous page) at the Royal
Vauxhall Tavern. This pub, in the London
district of Vauxhall, was one of several which
became well-known for their drag shows
during the boom enjoyed by this bizarre form of
entertainment in the 1970s. Although a
handful of houses achieved particular
reputations, a great many pubs began to
specialize in drag shows.*

*JAZZ is a perennial pub attraction, rooted
deeply in the tradition of locally-nurtured
entertainment, despite the regular presence of
American star names. Several pubs have
become synonymous with jazz, though the
listings in Melody Maker and Time Out
magazine change as pubs vary their musical
tone. In the cosmopolitan London district of
Earls Court, the Coleherne (right) has
enjoyed some popularity and a freewheeling
clientele over the years.*

said: 'They may be doing more for the future of English poetry and drama than they, or anyone else, thought possible in their most sanguine moments.' But a comeback in the changed social climate of the post-war period, faded as the 'music pubs' established themselves. A group called the Barrow Poets was subsidized by the Whitbread brewery company – renewing its links with the arts – in the 1960s and early 1970s. That, too, suffered, from the problems of performing for an audience which was not always willing to sit in silence.

Pictorial art poses no such difficulties. When Whitbread launched a patronage system in 1936, showing Royal Academy exhibitors in several pubs, drinkers appeared to enjoy discussing the pictures over their pints. Although the Whitbread scheme has long gone, publicans do exhibit pictures occasionally and art students have been known to hang work in their locals.

The most successful forms of entertainment in pubs are those which are lively and involving. An astonishing variety of music is performed in pubs, especially in big cities. There have been rare evenings of appropriate music at London's *Gilbert and Sullivan*, in the Strand, near the Savoy Theatre, where the comic operas were first performed. In the Irish neighbourhoods of inner London – on the North and West sides of town – music is a loud and continuous feature of pub life, especially at weekends. In the districts jocularly named County Camden Town and County Kilburn, pubs like the *Dublin Castle* and the *Belmont* have added concert rooms to cater for these performances. Perhaps because Irish immigrants to the United States influenced the growth of country-and-western music, that genre is also popular in Celtic neighbourhoods. In Hammersmith, a huge Victorian pub was re-named *The Nashville*, and established as a showplace for visiting American country musicians. Meanwhile, steel-band music and reggae thump out from the pubs in the Black neighbourhoods of North-West and South London. The *Atlantic*, in Coldharbour Lane, is particularly popular with inhabitants of Brixton, the biggest Black neighbourhood.

The pub music of each area reflects its population. Along the East Anglian coast there are a dozen or so pubs in which songs originating from the crews of Thames sailing barges have become a frequent spontaneous entertainment. In the Pennine valleys, it is not unknown for villagers to break into formal song, with parts for bass and tenor, soprano and contralto. The music of the North inspired the American songwriter Henry Clay Work, author of *Marching Through Georgia*. Resting one day at the *George*, on the Yorkshire–Durham border, he found himself humming in time to the grandfather clock which was ticking away in the corner. Words began to form in his mind, and a tune. He sat down and wrote his second famous song: 'My grandfather's clock was too large for the shelf, so it stood 90 years on the floor.'

Clearly, the English pub is an unselective muse . . . for the American wrote several temperance songs.

The English Inn
Gastronomy and the pub

I T WAS A SMALL achievement, but a significant one. In 1975, the *Black Bull*, a pub in rural North Yorkshire, won the *Mouton Cadet* menu competition. The joint winner was a major hotel in London with an international kitchen staff. It could be argued from that moment that the gastronomic revival of the English pub had become a recognized fact.

The same year, the *Good Food Guide* started a section dealing with pubs, listing almost 250 houses in England. The *Guide* had always mentioned pubs with their own separate dining rooms, but the new section was more concerned with places where casual drinking and casual eating could go hand-in-hand in the bars. The *Black Bull*, at Moulton, fits into both categories. Although its principal role today is as a restaurant, it continues to operate also as a pub. Customers can book a meal in one of its dining-rooms, or drop by for a casual drink in the bar, possibly with a snack of oysters or terrine. The *Guinea*, off Berkeley Square, is an even better example of this. The majority of people who visit the pub go for the Young's beer, and have no intention of visiting the adjoining room which houses, as part of the same establishment, one of London's most expensive restaurants.

Some gastronomic pubs, like the *Miner's Arms*, in Priddy, Somerset, have become wholly restaurants. This is sad. The *Miner's* brews its own beer, but you cannot go there only for a drink; the place is open solely to diners. The same applies to the *George and Vulture*, in the City of London, which was originally a pub, and is mentioned as such in *Pickwick Papers*. To redress the balance in part, Fleet Street's *Printer's Pie* used to be a restaurant, but later opened also as a pub, with some excellent beers.

Some Central London pubs, and many inns in the middle of country towns, offer substantial sit-down meals in their regular bars. The food is often quite traditionally English in a solid, but acceptable, way. Other pubs offer hot or cold snacks, of qualities varying from the imaginative to the appalling, to eat in the hand

THE LUNCHEON BAR, a phenomenon of the mid and late 1800s, depicted by a cartoonist of the period (above). Luncheon bars preceded the widespread introduction of the 'restaurant' from Continental Europe. Few recognizable luncheon bars survive, but Whitelock's (preceding page) is a fine Late Victorian example in Leeds, Yorkshire. The spirit of an earlier institution, the chop-house, is perhaps maintained by the Cheshire Cheese (facing page), in Fleet Street, London. The costumed cellar-guide has gone, but the establishment's history is inescapable. Some luncheon bars and chop-houses became restaurants; others, like Whitelock's and the Cheshire Cheese, developed into pubs.
Thus the luncheon bar and the chop-house, like the ale-house, the tavern, the inn, and the gin-shop, made their contributions to the evolution of The English Pub.

or on the knee. Others, far too many, offer cold sausages or worse – or nothing at all.

Many of the pubs singled out for their snacks and light meals in the *Good Food Guide* were also identified in the quite separate publication produced by the Campaign for Real Ale, detailing houses which sell traditionally-served beers. Not only were gourmets beginning to accept pubs as eating places, but – much more important – drinkers were beginning to expect good food. The long campaign in the gastronomic desert, the battle with the curly sandwich, the gristly pie and the tedious chicken-in-the-basket, had entered a new phase.

Just as English food has had its ups and downs, so pubs' attitude towards eating has been marked by vicissitudes. Drinking makes you hungry, and eating makes you thirsty, and both sets of circumstances are accompanied by considerable stimulation of the stomach. Neither aspect of this two-sided proposition has escaped the English publican, but his attention has wandered from time to time over the ages. In Saxon times, an ale-house might also have been a bakery, with the wife making the drink while her husband attended to the bread; inns were for centuries as much places in which to eat as they were places in which to drink or sleep. On the other hand, beer itself was considered to be as much a food as a drink. The truth of this conception is borne-out by the beer-drinker's belly. Because alcohol can supply a fifth of the energy the body needs, the beer-drinker who cut out those foods which he has replaced with beer would display less evidence of his past pleasures.

One way in which the relationship between eating and drinking can be resolved is to cook in beer. Although the Brewers' Society and companies like Guinness have occasionally publicized recipes using beer, few were as fitted to consumption in pubs as Shakespeare's 'roasted crabs that hiss in the pot.' These would, in fact, have been crab apples destined for a popular ale-based food-drink known as Lambswool. A London executive claims to breakfast on a similar concoction. He beats-up an egg, unsalted butter, nutmeg and brown sugar in half a pint of warmed draught mild. His wife says, with some ambivalence, that this 'tastes better than ordinary beer.'

Eating in ale-houses, inns, taverns and pubs has followed the fortunes of English cuisine, which probably reached its peak when the Age of Exploration, and the colonial era which followed, brought home exotic new foodstuffs and spices. The growth of trade and communications that accompanied the Industrial Revolution, and the emergence of a new monied class, made for splendid dining tables. The *nouveau riche* emulated the gargantuan appetites of the landed gentry, and their attitude was reflected in the fare offered by some of the most successful inns and taverns.

London hostelries in the 18th century were renowned for

Ye Olde Cheshire Cheese

Edward Thomas Hale, Licensed to sell by Retail intoxicating Liquor to be consumed On or Off the premises. Licensed to sell Tobacco.

Under 15 Sovere

Ye Olde
Cheshire Chee
Rebuilt 1667
in the reign of Charles
and continued successiv
in the Reigns of
James II   1685-16
Interregnum Dec.11.1688-Feb.15.16
William III & Mary II 1689-17
Anne   1702-17
George I   1714-172
George II   1727-176
George III   1760-182
George IV   1820-183
William IV   1830-183
Victoria   1837-19
Edward VII   1901-191
George V   1910-193
Edward VIII   1936
George VI   1936-195
Elizabeth II   1952

FOR LICENSED VICTUALLERS.
By Cuisinier.

*PUBLICANS in their more pompous moments
affect to describe themselves flatteringly as
'licensed victuallers.' This is a description
which they clearly viewed with some
earnestness at the turn of the century. In order
that they might live up to their gastronomic
obligations, their trade newspaper of the
period carried a cookery column by 'Cuisinier.'
The newspaper was called, of course . . .
'The Licensed Victualler's Gazette.'*

their food. The turtle soup and oysters, the fine roast meats and game, were the envy of the French, who started their own imitations of the English inn in Paris. A song celebrating the steak-and-kidney pudding served at the *Cheshire Cheese*, in Fleet Street, trumpets, 'we scorned all foreign fare . . . true British food was there.' To be pedantic, the flamboyant pudding has its origins in the Norman pottage, a more humble, porridge-like concoction of meat and cereals. But when the pottage evolved into the pudding, it became a central, and elevated, theme in English cooking.

Dr Johnson so much enjoyed the pudding at the *Cheshire Cheese* that one was sent to his birthday party in his home town of Lichfield, in the Midlands. Today's pudding at the *Cheese* no longer contains larks and oysters, but it does contain game, and the pub serves excellent Burton beer. Every year, in mid-October, a celebrity is summoned to the *Cheese* to cut a portion and open a new 'pudding season'; during the summer, the dish is replaced on the menu by a pie, also of steak-and-kidney. Perhaps in the hope of tempting drinkers to open their cheque-books at the dining tables, the *Cheshire Cheese* serves no snacks in the bar.

Country inn-keepers were also building reputations in the 18th century. In Lancashire, the energetic Elizabeth Raffald contrived to write the classic cookery book *The Experienced English Housekeeper* while also running three inns and a confectionery shop and giving birth to 16 daughters. No doubt the daughters added to the pleasures of meals at her establishments as they brought forth delicate potted char (a rare fish from the Lake District), fried oysters, roast lobster and marbled veal, all washed down with strong Northern beer.

At the same *White Hart* favoured by Thomas Paine, in Lewes, Sussex, the cuisine of William Verrall became a great attraction. In his book, Verrall identified himself as 'no more than what is vulgarly called a poor publican,' but his recipes testify that this was false modesty. His partridge pie with endive, or turkey braised with chestnuts, must have gone down well in Regency Lewes. He also paved the way for more recent publicans in serving 'foreign food.' His macaroni cheese – a dish he appears to have introduced to England – sounds a good deal more appetising, with its herbs, spices, parmesan, orange and lemon juice, than the tasteless product sometimes served up in pubs today.

By the mid 19th century, the tables seem to have turned. French food was becoming sufficiently fashionable in England for Dr William Kitchiner, author of *The Cook's Oracle*, to pour scorn on English epicures who could 'not endure the sight of the best bill of fare unless it was written in pretty good bad French.' Eventually, the moralistic attitudes of the Victorians towards any sort of sensual enjoyment coloured their attitude towards extravagance in the kitchen. If the arbiters of social behaviour

ALL IN THE FAMILY . . .

SOME of the good things in life are rare . . . the unspoiled countryside, for example, and English oysters. Such pleasures can still be enjoyed at the *Plough and Sail*, at Snape, Suffolk. The world has changed since the early 1930s, when the painting above was published by the *Tatler*, but the pub retains its character. The drinkers depicted by artist T. C. Dugdale may have gone, but their sons and nephews were still there when the photograph on the right was taken in 1975. The *Plough and Sail* is typical of East Anglia's attractive waterside pubs. The lakes, rivers and estuaries of Anglia provide distinctive scenery, sailing and seafood. The *Plough and Sail* itself sometimes offers oysters, for example. There is music, too. The building behind the pub is the former maltings which now serves as a concert hall for the fashionable Aldeburgh Festival each year in June, brainchild of composer Benjamin Britten.

did not condemn themselves to 'wholesome' and tasteless eating, they certainly downgraded the dining customs of children and servants, thus inflicting permanent damage on the gastronomic sensibilities of the English. Nor did the culinary specialities of the English countryside stand much chance of survival so long as the rural population was being sucked into labour and deprivation in the growing industrial cities.

An exciting moment of revival in hostelry cooking was brought about in the 1920s and 1930s by John Fothergill, who is said to have 'done for the English inn what Boulestin did for the London restaurant.' A classical scholar and author, friend of Oscar Wilde and Augustus John, Fothergill ran three inns, the most famous of which was the *Spreadeagle*, at Thame, in Oxford-shire. His cooking was genuinely creative, and recipes such as mauve soup seemed to fit the gay and brittle spirit of the period.

If the coaching inn had been killed by the birth of the railways, then the growth of motoring in the post-war period of prosperity gave a new life to many country pubs, dozens of which became fashionable weekend eating places for the new gen-eration of car-owners. The Elizabeth Raffalds and William Verralls had their modern equivalents: Mrs Fisher, at the *Black Horse*, Grimsthorpe, Lincolnshire, won considerable renown for her classical English cooking; at the *Duck Inn*, Pett Bottom, Kent, Ulla Laing, Swedish wife of the proprietor, set a lively imag-ination to work on both traditional and international fare. Fothergill's mantle was perhaps inherited by J. H. de la Tickell, of the *Tickell Arms*, Whittlesford, Cambridgeshire. This zanily-run pub, much favoured by Cambridge University people, became known for game pies and wholemeal bread, accom-panied by beer from the wood and classical music.

Locally-baked bread has added appetite-appeal to the sandwiches at the *Horse and Groom*, a useful resting-place after a walk on London's Hampstead Heath. Other pubs have become popular because they bake their own bread: *The Inn*, at Fresh-ford, Wiltshire; the *Blacksmith's Arms*, at Elm, Cambridgeshire;

THE DINING TABLE . . . sitting down for a midday meal in the main bar of a London pub during the early 1950s. Hardly Palm Court, but not quite a corner 'caff,' either. The random nature of the accoutrements perfectly fits the pub idiom. A random menu, too, for bar-snack diners at the Crown (right), in Ashton, near Stoke Bruerne, Northamptonshire. Chips with everything, English-style hamburgers, and a couple of imports . . . eels, a speciality more common in London, and pickled eggs, more popular in the North. The shining pumps may not be in use, but the Crown is a splendidly eccentric pub in the heart of canal country.

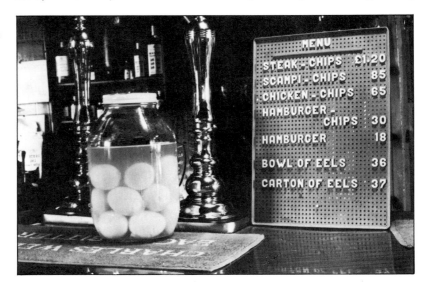

and the *Crown*, at Downham Market, Norfolk, have won honourable mention. The *Hobnails Inn*, at Little Washbourne, Gloucestershire, has been known to offer nearly 50 different fillings in its rolls. Just as the fresh-bread pubs challenge that highly-dispensable English tradition of the curly sandwich, so such a variety of fillings makes for nice eating when you can get it. The English sandwich has its moments of substance when caring Northern publicans coat thick slices of beef or cheese in home-pickled onions (Northerners like pickling things, and pubs are particularly fond of selling pickled eggs from great jars). There are no guides to such delights, nor to much of what is best in pub food, but an exploration of the pickled egg belt – girdling the cities of Hull, Liverpool and Newcastle – is an experience in itself. For more luxurious fillings, the areas round salmon rivers like the Tweed and the Severn hold the occasional delight.

Over-sophistication, on the other hand, is a grave danger. Cheeses, for example, have increasingly been imported from wine-growing countries. Brie and Dolcelatte may flatter the taste of people who have toyed with foreign habits while on holiday, but England has plenty of French and Italian restaurants for that sort of thing. Cheddar, but only of a good tangy quality, is the ideal cheese to eat with bread and beer. It isn't always easy to find good cheddar, since cheese has been affected as badly as beer by creeping blandness. When *The Guardian* launched its watchdog column on beer, writer Richard Boston soon extended his attentions to cheese. It is a product which seems to bring out the worst in those licensees, or pub-owning companies, whose insensitivity towards food and drink is matched only by their behaviour towards the English language. Anyone who dare not serve bread and cheese without referring to it as a 'Ploughman's Lunch' is unlikely to care, or know, much about the quality of his offerings. Good cheddar, however, can still be found, and its native country around the Avon and Somerset is as good a place as any in which to look for the cheese at its best.

Another classic English cheese which goes well in a sandwich with a pint of beer is Stilton, which gets its name indirectly from a pub. Although the cheese originates from the Midland county of Leicestershire, its name arises from the more Easterly village of Stilton. The farmers used to take their cheese to an inn at Stilton, which was on the old Great North Road, for distribution farther afield. Good Stilton is widely available, but some gastronomes prefer the blue-veined Wensleydale, which is far more seldom seen. Sightings have been reported at the *Bluebell*, Kettlewell, North Yorkshire, and the *Bay Horse*, Winton, Cumbria.

While many regional cheeses have vanished, and those like Suffolk – reputed to have made dogs bark – may be no loss, the search for survivors can involve some enjoyable pub-crawling. People still go looking for Dorset Blue Vinney as if it were the

Holy Grail. In fact, this hard cheese, no longer commercially available, would meet with the approval of few people if it were offered anonymously; it has been made desirable only by its scarcity. Although there are still people in the county who make it, careless visitors are satisfied with a full-cream veined cheese called Dorset Blue. This is a more recent cheese, created to exploit the mystique, and of extremely erratic quality. At its worst, it is scarcely worth eating; at its best, it is creamily memorable. The *Wise Man*, at West Stafford, near Dorchester, has been known to offer a fine specimen. In order perhaps to preserve the aura of the original, the licensee hazily declines to remember where he buys his cheese.

Among cream cheeses, such regional splendours as Slipcote, Cottenham and Cambridge seem to have gone for good, but mourners can staunch their tears at the *Rose and Thistle*, Rockbourne, Hampshire. That splendid establishment makes its own cream cheese, as well as serving locally-smoked trout.

Fish is served in a good number of pubs, as indeed it should be in a country with such a high proportion of coastline. No part of England is more than 60 miles from the sea, and the green and pleasant hills – not to mention the craggier ones – water every

'COME DINE with the Lobster, the Oyster and me' . . . a delightful pastiche of Lewis Carroll was published by Guinness in 1933. The work was beautifully illustrated, with acknowledgments to Tenniel and others, and its witty allusions to Guinness could hardly have offended even the purists among Carroll devotees. Oysters are very happily accompanied by either Guinness or Black Velvet. Lobster, too, is sometimes available at the more ambitious country pubs.

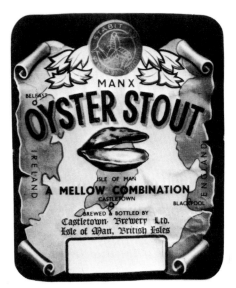

A GOURMET TREAT for offshore drinkers evaporated when Castletown Brewery, on the Isle of Man, stopped producing Oyster Stout, in the late 1960s. The beer, which contained oyster concentrate, was exported to the United States, Asia and Africa. The Isle of Man is still good drinking country: the quality of its brews is protected by a Pure Beer Act, and its pub-opening hours are longer than those in England. After a few days sampling Lancashire's excellent beers (and fish suppers), a day or two's outing to the Isle of Man makes a grand finale to a North-Western pub-crawl.

county with rivers. Whitebait are one of London's traditional dishes because they once swam up the Thames in considerable quantity. The taverns around Greenwich used to have a considerable upsurge in popularity during the whitebait season, and freezing has allowed these tasty little fish to be included again on menu cards.

Similarly, eels have been a London favourite for centuries, as well as having enjoyed some popularity in other parts of the country. Not only did the phallic connotations of this slippery, muscular and elongated fish give it a reputation as an aphrodisiac; its ability to survive out of water enabled it to be transported alive over long distances, and so offered absolutely fresh. After being a working-class food for 100 years, eels became chic in the mid-1970s. The traditional London speciality of eels cooked, allowed to cool in their own jelly and served from special stalls, makes a splendidly indigestible post-pub snack to eat in the street. It is almost as robust as Northern fish and chips, eaten out of the football-results edition of a Saturday evening newspaper.

One enterprising Cockney took his eels with him when he went into energetic retirement in a Northamptonshire country pub. Visitors to the *Crown Inn*, at Ashton, were surprised to see eels in a tank, available to be cooked and served at the pub in a variety of styles. The *Crown* of eels is at the Ashton near Stoke Bruerne, not the one near Oundle where, accompanied by much drinking, the international Conker Championships are held.

Young eels, like crystalline bootlaces, are still eaten along the Severn estuary during April, though the creatures' annual migration to the Sargasso Sea has been somewhat uncertain in recent years. Like so many other esoteric specialities, the young eels – known as elvers – shun food guides, and require pursuit with persistence and luck. Drinkers with both of these qualities may chance upon elvers fried with egg in pubs between Bristol and Gloucester. If the search proves tiring, a glass of hot cider with ginger may conceivably be procured as a pick-me-up.

English oysters, particularly the small but delicious Whitstable and Colchester Natives, have become scarce and expensive since the beds were decimated by disease in the 19th century. Once they were so profuse that they had little value – Dickens said oysters and poverty went together (the same went for salmon). Oysters' use in cooking, particularly with steak-and-kidney pudding has all but disappeared – sometimes mussels are substituted. Steak-and-kidney pudding with oysters has, however, continued to be served in winter at the *King's Head*, at Orford, Suffolk. Other pubs to win note for their oysters have been the *Plough and Sail*, at Snape, Suffolk, serving them as 'angels on horseback' (wrapped in a slice of bacon and grilled), and the *White Hart*, at Coggeshall, Essex.

The men who occasionally set up stall outside pubs to sell

The Old "DANIEL LAMBERT" as rebuilt in 1891 Hotel & Tavern
10 & 12, Ludgate Hill, & 2 & 3, Ave Maria Lane.

MR BARNES THE PROPRIETOR

MAIN ENTRANCE LUDGATE HILL

THE SALOON BAR. ENTRANCE FROM LUDGATE HILL.

THE PORTRAIT OF DANIEL LAMBERT WHO DIED 1809 AGED 39 & WEIGHED 52 ST.

IN THE GRILL ROOM

THE GROWTH of restaurants, cafés and clubs in the second half of the 1800s led to the temporary abandonment of pubs by the middle classes towards the end of the century. Those pubs which retained their respectability were the ones which emphasized their function as restaurants. The Daniel Lambert, in London's Ludgate Hill, was one such establishment. With both a saloon bar and a grill-room, it had more than enough dignity to maintain its social standing, as evidenced by this extravagant advertisement, from the Daily Graphic of 1891.

shellfish, or call into the bar with a basket full, are a happy hangover from Victorian days, when street-trading was so prevalent that fried-fish vendors and itinerant piemen were a major source of drinking men's snacks. Pie-selling was traditionally something of a gamble, as pub customers would toss a penny, and require the vendor to call heads or tails. If the pieman won the toss, he kept the penny; if he lost, the customer got a free snack. 'Tossing the pieman' was a sport among the richer and more intoxicated customers, irrespective of whether they were hungry. It often ended in a rumbustious pie-throwing battle in which the vendor was a likely target – and Hollywood comedians the subsequent benefactors.

While many pubs serve hot pies of one sort or another, to eat with a knife and fork, the popular cold pie is easier to handle during serious drinking. Although questionable concoctions from the big food corporations have spread like a plague, every region has its own local forms of pie, pasty or similar. Whether the pies are big (and served by the slice) or small (and sold complete), they are usually made with pork, occasionally with game, beef, or mutton.

Melton Mowbray, in Leicestershire, has the best-known pork pie, which should properly be flavoured with a hint of anchovy. These pies are available in pubs in the area, and beyond. Good Cornish pasties can only easily be found in the Duchy, where they are sometimes known by the Cornish-

Post-drink snack, outside the Queen's Head, in Ramsgate, Kent . . . the Londoner's traditional delicacy, at one of his favourite resorts.

language name of Tiddy Oggy. They were once made with pilchards, but are today made with meat and potato. The *Rising Sun*, at St Mawes, has a reputation for the genuine article; it also has a restaurant for visitors who want something more substantial. The *Blue Anchor*, at Helston, offers pasties with home-brewed beer. Another popular variant on the meat-and-pastry theme is the sausage roll. The *Red Lion*, on the Romney Marsh at Margate, Kent, makes its own sausage rolls. It also sells splendid cakes to the tea-shop next door, perhaps to compensate for the fact that the pub uses the shop as a venue for dart-games.

What might be described as 'folk foods' crop up all over England. The *Red Lion*, at Snodland, Kent, offers pease pudding and faggots (meats like liver, chopped, seasoned and baked) on Saturday lunchtimes. In the North-West, there is talk of 'Stew and Hard' (oatcakes and brawn) at the *Gaits Inn*, Blacko, near Nelson, Lancashire. Then there is steak and cow-heel pie at the *Bells*, at Peover, in Cheshire (shades of Mr Codlin, in Dickens' *Old Curiosity Shop*, who enjoyed a stew of tripe, cow-heel, bacon, steak and vegetables at the *Jolly Sandboys*). In the North-East, ham, pease pudding and stotty cake are a fitting accompaniment to music-hall entertainment at the *White Mare Pool*, Felling, near Newcastle.

Traditional dishes like parsley pie and tipsy parson are on an *haute cuisine* menu at the *Old Inn*, Drewsteignton, on the edge of Dartmoor, along with more internationally-recognized dishes. Chinese food has been known to enter the English pub, notably at the *Salisbury Arms*, in Hertford, and in the same county at the *Volunteer*, Waltham Abbey. Austrian dishes have been featured at the *Manchester Regiment*, in that city's district of Hulme Hall; there is a Swiss-style restaurant at the *Coach and Horses*, Trumpington, Cambridgeshire; and the *Yew Tree*, Salisbury, has its own brand of robust Northern French cuisine.

Such places, and a great many more, are the exotic exception. The growing flirtation with food has not seduced the English pub away from its main roles in life as a place for drinking and talking. Even inducements to those pleasures are not always present. Gone, regrettably, are the days when salty titbits like lark's tongues, anchovies, red herrings and even caviare were commonly offered free of charge on the bars of London taverns as 'pullers-on', or thirst-makers. These days, only pubs with cocktail bars are likely to offer free snacks, and then rarely anything fancier than peanuts.

More often, the peanuts have to be paid for, like the almost universal bag of what the British call potato crisps and the Americans chips. It is hard today to believe that the crisp pioneer Smith had difficulty in persuading publicans to stock his product. Crisp-eaters left greasy marks on glasses, which were difficult to clean in pre-detergent days.

Food is fine . . . but it must not be allowed to blemish the drinking.

The Living Local
Social change and the pub

WHEN ENGLAND presents itself to the world at large, the image usually includes a pub. The English film classics of the 1940s, *Mrs Miniver* and beyond, always seemed to feature a pub among their studio sets. It appeared forever to be the same pub: a reassuring haven where the middle-class people who dominated the storyline could patronize with a kind word and a half-pint, their gardeners and other such menials, safe in the knowledge that working people had hearts of gold.

Perhaps the whole English film industry drank in the same local. All the famous studios (evocative closing-title names like Ealing and Elstree) were on the green fringes of London, where the cosily-named Home Counties spawn small country towns and villages, inhabited largely by commuters. Towns and villages in Thames Valley counties like Berkshire and Oxfordshire still have their English-movie locals, where stockbrokers can tighten their belts and recall the days when people knew their rightful place in society. But there always was another, bigger England, with occasionally more abrasive textures, and grittier pubs.

England has so many typical pubs – all typical, and all different. There are cosy pubs, and bare ones. Often, the bare ones – not having become distracted with decor – have better beer. Paradoxically, the bare ones are more comfortable, too, because they are not encumbered with pretensions. It is no longer normal for pubs to scatter sawdust into which their patrons may spit, but plenty of pubs survive which deserve the affectionate epithet 'spit-and-sawdust.' A fine example is the *Lamb and Flag*, in Covent Garden, dubbed 'The Bucket of Blood' ever since Dryden was mugged there.

The typical pub can be the 17th-century house in the City of London, or the Edwardian palace in Liverpool; the 'smugglers' pub' boasted by every coastal village (especially in the West), or

That old, familiar haven . . . Oxfordshire pub in the early 1950s

HORSEPOWER is retained by several brewers. Some even reintroduced horses during the early 1970s, after time-and-motion studies had proved them to be more cost-effective than trucks on home-town deliveries. In the East of England, Adnams' (above) still use horses. So do Sam Smith's, in the North. The Sam Smith team on the facing page, delivering to a house in York, are stabled at a pub in the same city, called the Shire Horse. Other Northern brewers using horses include Vaux, of Sunderland, and Thwaites', of Blackburn. In the West, Courage's use horses for Plymouth deliveries. In London, Young's and Whitbread maintain the tradition.

the canalside pub (especially in Midland counties like Northamptonshire and Warwickshire); the thatched pub in Dorset, or the timbered inn at Tewkesbury or Ledbury, Shrewsbury or Chester; the rugged hillside local in the Pennines, or the austere boozer for mighty beer-drinkers among the shipyards of the rivers Tyne, Wear and Tees.

The pub at its best may be a place for drinking and talking (or, better still, for talking and drinking), but it can also be a place for eating, for games and sports, for music (jukebox or live, all tastes catered for), for striptease, or drag, or theatre. It can be any of these things, or a little of each, so long as it remains a pub. To be a pub, it must cater for those people who want nothing more than a drink; it must serve them at regular prices, and without charging for entry. When the inns of Elizabethan times became preoccupied with their stage performances, they spun-off the theatre as a separate institution. When the Victorian music-hall outgrew the pub, it also spun-off.

The pub survives, as a permanent and resilient institution in English community life. An Englishman may rarely have cause to visit his town hall, he may never visit his local church (or any other), but the local pub is a different matter. Every other Englishman has an intimate knowledge of at least one neighbourhood pub, and possibly another near his place of work. Unlike the church, the pub has hardly been sacrosanct, notwithstanding its being the object of such devotions. On the other hand, the continuity of communities has protected the public house where a private home might more readily be demolished after a lifetime or two. Only in the last three or four decades has the pub felt the full force of delinquent 'developers,' and that outbreak of violence has finally squeezed recognition from architectural snobs that pubs can be buildings of some historical importance. The trouble with pubs has been that they are so easily taken for granted.

The pub enters the consciousness of the Englishman years before he can enter the pub. (Unless the pub has a special place for children – the few that do are likely to advertise the fact – the house cannot admit anyone under 14, nor serve anyone under 18. Since Britain, unlike other allegedly-free countries, does not force people to carry identity cards, the latter rule is frequently flouted by young customers, but rarely with the knowledge of the licensee.)

The pub is the place that children's fathers get shouted at by children's mothers for having dallied in. The pub is a landmark in conversation: something happened outside the *Rose and Crown;* turn left at the *King Charles;* park your car 100 yards past the *Star and Garter.* Pub is a three-letter word that serves so many purposes. The pub is the place where there is a wooden trapdoor in the pavement. Sometimes, especially in the mornings, the trapdoor is opened, to receive casks, rolling down a ramp. On such

occasions, the pub is a parking-place for boldly-painted trucks, and sometimes horses pulling drays. (The London brewery of Young's is just one which has retained horse-power.) The pub is the place where lights shine through translucent glass in the evenings, the doors swing open to exhale noisy conversation and beery smells. The pub is the place where stubble-chinned school-boys sneak in plain clothes to prove their manliness; anyone can fool around with girls, but only real men drink in pubs.

The machismo of the pub has mercifully subsided, though it is still primarily a male domain. Even the gay pubs are usually for male homosexuals, and never for women. Few women would hesitate to go into a pub if they had arranged to meet a man friend there, but many would shrink from drinking alone. Brewers' attempts to make their houses attractive to women, and to couples, have nonetheless caused great damage. Pubs should not be trivialized, nor should they be euphemized. The sexual in-clinations of lavatories should not, for example, be identified with such terms as 'Lads' and 'Lasses' or 'Knights' and 'Damsels.' Such window-dressing is as offensive to the honest pub-goer as decoration with reproduction horse-brasses, a habit which has discredited those publicans who collect the real thing.

Why publicans should accumulate objects is another question. Perhaps the habit started in the days of the Saxon alehouse, when the implements of brewing may have hung on the wall, perhaps keeping company with the equipment of kitchen and bakehouse and the tools of the land. Pewter tankards and pot vessels may have first filled decorative shelves when their function was usurped by glasses; today, toby-jugs are collected by publicans all over the country. Chamber-pots are a vulgar variation on the theme, practised by many pubs. Such a coarse habit seems particularly appropriate to bucolic counties like Wiltshire, where, in the village of Wootton Bassett, a collection of chamber pots has been assembled at the *Borough Arms*. Any odd antiquity qualifies as being worthy of collection by publicans, plus such ephemera as unusual banknotes, ties (of regiments or clubs), car-pennants, matchboxes and the like.

Antiquities don't have to feature in collections. A staircase from Fotheringay Castle was installed in the *Talbot Hotel*, at Oundle, Northamptonshire, while the *Roman Bath*, at York, gets its name from the original use to which its cellar was put. Not far away at Kirby Wiske, near Thirsk, in North Yorkshire, is a pub called the *Busby Stoop*, named after a man who was hanged there. Busby seems to have left a curse on the place. According to local legend, anyone who sits on a certain chair in the pub will die violently. The last four people to have sat in the chair are said to have died in accidents. Serious drinkers, of course, imbibe while standing up – the beer goes down better that way, and any risk of imminent death is minimised. Only women sit down in pubs.

Ghosts adopt a wider variety of postures, and one even takes his dog to the *White Swan*, in Birmingham. Dogs are popular in pubs, often reaching up to the bar, drinking out of glasses on the floor, and performing other such questionable tricks. It is a sad reflection on Englishmen that even ghosts affect to be taking the dog for a walk when they are really popping out for a quick pint. So many pubs find a resident ghost to be a necessity that an entire volume on *Haunted Inns* has been written by Marc Alexander.

One of the best-known among such establishments is the *George and Dragon*, at West Wycombe, Buckinghamshire, which apparently cannot call upon its patron saint for protection against the ghostly memories of the orgiastic 18th-century Hellfire Club. Across the county border in Bedfordshire, the *Chequers*, at Wootton, offers a ghost, and such phenomena allegedly occur in pubs all the way from the South-East to the North-West, where the *Stork*, at Billinge, near Wigan, seems an unlikely a location as any.

THE SHIPYARDS, coal-mines and steelworks of the Tyne, Wear and Tees region have bred their own wry strain of drinking man, his self-mocking humour nurtured by the rigours and uncertainties of employment in the region. The locally-conceived but internationally-syndicated cartoon character Andy Capp is famous for his drinking habits. His name is a pun both on the working man's traditional cap, and the North-East's passion for sport. (For Andy Capp, read 'handicap,' in the racing of horses, dogs or pigeons.) The pubscape above could only be in the North-East. The Albion overlooks the docks at the mouth of the Wear, in Sunderland.

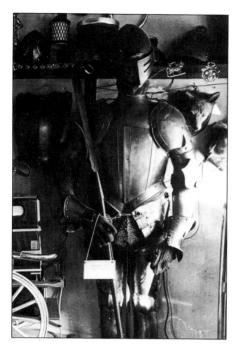

THE COLLECTORS: The Wise Man (facing page), near Dorchester, has a fine display of Toby jugs, the most popular items in pub collections. A more random delight in accumulation is suggested by the selection at the Crown, in Ashton, near Stoke Bruerne, Northamptonshire (above). Collections in pubs range from china to stuffed animals, from railway ephemera to marine mementoes.

Whether Orwell ever came across that particular ghost is not recorded, but he shared the interest which so many writers have manifested in the public house as an institution. He was less concerned with spirits than draught stout, a drink the rarity of which he bemoaned. Orwell raised this question in the London *Evening Standard* of February 9, 1946, and his point was taken up by the same paper almost 30 years later, on August 26, 1975. On this occasion, columnist Alan Watkins correctly pointed out that draught stout was now relatively common, and so were pubs with gardens, another of Orwell's concerns. The pub has changed, but not always for the worse.

Orwell's ideal pub also had motherly barmaids. Although he did not go into this, there are two basic types of barmaid: surrogate mothers, and surrogate bedmates. The types are quite distinct, though the pub-goer who drinks too much may eventually confuse them, especially if the barmaid in question is of the buxom mould characteristic to her occupation. Not only does beer inflame lust if taken to excess: heavy-beer drinkers are often male-chauvinists. In the days when Nice Girls Didn't, it was popularly thought that barmaids did, though this was not always the case. Now that Nice Girls are out of style, so are blousy barmaids. Happily, there are still a few pubs which bulge with anachronisms.

With rarity, comes value; a maxim which might be applied to many aspects of the pub. Where the Englishman once chose his pub on the basis of its proximity to his home, perhaps also taking into account his compatibility with its regular customers (which cannot always be assumed), he may today weigh further considerations. Although the *Good Beer Guide* is an invaluable briefing, only extensive first-hand sampling will satisfy the keen pub-goer. Experience is quickly gained, and this sort of pursuit is a very enjoyable way to mis-spend a lifetime, as many an Englishman has discovered.

Since the beer is the first essential, though only the first, it is always interesting to try a house belonging to a local brewer. Even if the beer turns out to be terrible, at least the style of the pub was not conceived for national consumption by someone in a distant London office. Once having entered a pub, there is no obligation to stay for a drink if the place looks dreadful inside. On the other hand, a sudden hush in the bar may merely indicate that the locals are curious (Northerners frequently experience this on deserting their own friendly counties for the less warm social climes of the South). Hand-pumps on the bar are obviously a good sign, but it is important to make sure that they are actually being used. Sometimes they are merely left there for decoration, and occasionally they are fakes which actuate some more questionable mechanism. The genuine beer-engine does require a slight effort on the part of the puller, and a gently pumping action, producing half a pint per stroke. Beer served by

SUNDAY LUNCHTIME . . . and the pub serves to stimulate the appetite for roast beef, with Yorkshire pudding, or to soothe the mind for an afternoon snooze. A shirtsleeve chat with neighbours, a weekly renewal of acquaintance, a few bottles to take home . . . the English Sunday has its own drowsy ritual. Near city pubs like the Old Pack Horse, in Chiswick, London, there's usually a newsvendor at hand to gild weekly gossip. In the country, such trifles are hardly needed at the Crooked Billet, in Stoke Row, Oxfordshire. On Sunday, the pub is a milestone to confirm a week completed. Could time pass without time being called?

thumb-taps directly from barrels behind the bar is preferred by rigid purists, but is rare in towns and cities. This method of serving can be faked, but only with considerable ingenuity.

That other sign of the traditional English pub, the fat and bluff landlord, all waistcoat and whiskers, may also be a fake. At least one such landlord in the 17th century, William Davis, doubled up as a highwayman. He was hanged outside his own pub, in Bagshot, Surrey. Today's landlord may not be a criminal, but he is often a rude bigot, with manners acquired in the Army or the colonies. London's *Pub of the Year* award in 1975 went to no such landlord, but to a pub run by a smiling-faced, Afro-haired Black landlady; the *Greyhound*, in Kensington Square. Considering that the pub was Thackeray's old local, the landlady flouted tradition somewhat by serving Harvey Wall-bangers and Bahama Mamas, not to mention meat-loaf and latkes. But it became a very popular place.

Such are the exotic distractions that can trap the seeker after pub perfection, but the snare should be avoided. A man who set a fine example, on his return from the United States, was the great radical William Cobbett. His account of *Rural Rides*, published in 1830, demonstrates not only a thorough interest in England's inns but also a ceaseless quest for new experiences. His reward: they named a pub after him in his birthplace of Farnham, Surrey. Cobbett knew the value of exploration at grass-roots, and there are no roots grassier than those of the English pub.

Those who love the institution will continue to investigate it. Because no two pubs are the same (despite the worst efforts of the big brewers), the search can never reach a conclusion. Therein lies its joy.

Index